KU-782-156

50 Walks in

BRECON BEACONS
& SOUTH WALES

First published 2003
Researched and written by Tom Hutton

Produced by AA Publishing
© Automobile Association Developments Limited 2003
Illustrations © Automobile Association Developments Limited 2003

Published by AA Publishing (a trading name of Automobile
Association Developments Limited, whose registered office is
Millstream, Maidenhead, Windsor, SL4 5GD;
registered number 1878835)

ISBN 0 7495 3622 5

A01300

A CIP catalogue record for this book is available
from the British Library.

The contents of this book are believed correct at the time of printing.
Nevertheless, the publishers cannot be held responsible for any errors
or omissions or for changes in the details given in this book or for
the consequences of any reliance on the information it provides. This
does not affect your statutory rights. We have tried to ensure
accuracy in this book, but things do change and we would be grateful
if readers would advise us of any inaccuracies they may encounter.

We have taken all reasonable steps to ensure that these walks are
safe and achievable by walkers with a realistic level of fitness.
However, all outdoor activities involve a degree of risk and the
publishers accept no responsibility for any injuries caused to
readers whilst following these walks. For more advice on walking
safely see page 128. The mileage range shown on the front cover is for
guidance only – some walks may exceed or be less than these
distances.

Visit the AA Publishing website at www.theAA.com

Paste-up and editorial by Outcrop Publishing Services Ltd, Cumbria
for AA Publishing

Colour reproduction by LC Repro
Printed in Italy by G Canale & C SPA, Torino, Italy

Legend

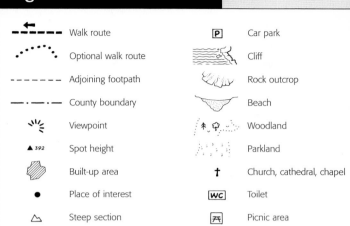

◄-▪-▪-▪-▪-	Walk route	P	Car park
••••••••	Optional walk route		Cliff
-------	Adjoining footpath		Rock outcrop
—·—·—·	County boundary		Beach
☼	Viewpoint		Woodland
▲ 392	Spot height		Parkland
	Built-up area	†	Church, cathedral, chapel
●	Place of interest	WC	Toilet
△	Steep section	🛆	Picnic area

Brecon Beacons & South Wales locator map

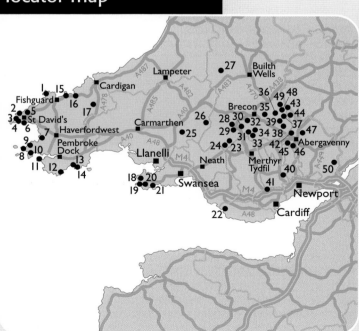

Contents
=====

Contents

Contents

Contents

Rating: Each walk is rated for its relative difficulty compared to the other walks in this book. Walks marked 🚶🚶 🚶 🚶 are likely to be shorter and easier with little total ascent. The hardest walks are marked 🚶🚶 🚶🚶 🚶🚶 .

Walking in Safety: For advice and safety tips ➤ 128.

Introducing Brecon Beacons & South Wales

There is no specific line on a map and there is no archetypal landscape or terrain that defines South Wales. More than anything, South Wales defines itself by its variety and its contrasts. From beach to mountain, cathedral to chapel, villain to saint and common to capital, the only parity is the disparity. The common thread is that they all have their beauties and they will all capture your imagination.

The majority of the walks in this book are centred on the area's two National Parks. For this I make no apologies. The Pembrokeshire Coast alone boasts over 180 miles (290km) of coast path, but this doesn't tell half the story. The history, adorned with myths and legends of saints and kings fills in some of the gaps, though it still says little about the wildlife. Seabirds, seals and porpoises vie for your attention, while falcons share the flower-carpeted cliff tops with a whole host of other creatures.

The Brecon Beacons National Park is very much my 'home range'. The central peaks, or the true 'Brecon Beacons', see the most adulation. As well as boasting the highest ground in Southern Britain, their tabletop summits preside over some of the finest upland scenery this country can offer. To the east, the Black Mountains are a hill-walkers paradise; their lumbering whaleback ridges and deeply cloven valleys are literally riddled with tracks and trails that make exploration both safe and easy. The two westernmost ranges, Fforest Fawr and the Black Mountain (singular), are a very different proposition, composed mainly of huge tracts of moorland which, on the whole, fall slightly outside the domain of this book. I have however, suggested some of the easier options available, including a tour of the incomparable Waterfall Country and a circuit around the formidable crags of the Carmarthen Fan.

With the remainder of the walks, I've tried to showcase other favourite images of South Wales. I've cherry-picked the best of the Gower Coast, visiting swaths of golden sand embedded in jagged limestone cliffs, and sampled a refreshingly beautiful stretch of the Glamorgan Heritage Coast – a hidden gem tucked away in a little-known corner.

No book on this region would be complete without a mention of the Valleys and, of course, the industries

PUBLIC TRANSPORT

Most of the walks in the book return to their original starting point. Unfortunately, these starting points are often in rural areas where there is little or no public transport. The three linear walks are connected by regular bus services, although this may vary at weekends, bank holidays and in the winter. For public transport details call 0870 608 2 608 and ask for the area you are visiting. Information is also available on the internet at www.pti.org.uk.

that formed their tightly knit communities. Few landscapes have altered more radically in recent decades and the revitalised hilltops now make for some surprisingly good walking. I've also touched on the capital, Cardiff, making an invigorating tour from a fairy-tale castle, just a few miles from the centre. Finally, I've stretched the region's boundaries as far as I could. To the north, I've included the austere charms of Abergwesyn Common, a definite walk on the wild side and once the last stand of the beautiful red kite. And east, to the border, to follow the lazy line of the meandering River Wye through some stunning deciduous woodland.

In compiling the walks I've seen and experienced much. I've been bombarded with giant hailstones on a remote mountaintop and watched dolphins and porpoises frolic against a fire-red sunset off the Pembrokeshire Coast. Every mile has been an honour and a privilege and I hope that it will feel the same way to you too.

Using this Book

Information panels

An information panel for each walk shows its relative difficulty (➤ 5), the distance and total amount of ascent. An indication of the gradients you will encounter is shown by the rating ⛰ ⛰ ⛰ (no steep slopes) to ⛰ ⛰ ⛰ (several very steep slopes).

Maps

There are 30 maps, covering 40 of the walks. Some walks have a suggested option in the same area. The information panel for these walks will tell you how much extra walking is involved. On short-cut suggestions the panel will tell you the total distance if you set out from the start of the main walk. Where an option returns to the same point on the main walk, just the distance of the loop is given. Where an option leaves the main walk at one point and returns to it at another, then the distance shown is for the whole walk. The minimum time suggested is for reasonably fit walkers and doesn't allow for stops. Each walk has a suggested map. Laminated aqua3 maps are longer lasting and water resistant.

Start Points

The start of each walk is given as a six-figure grid reference prefixed by two letters indicating which 100km square of the National Grid it refers to. You'll find more information on grid references on most Ordnance Survey maps.

Dogs

We have tried to give dog owners useful advice about how dog friendly each walk is. Please respect other countryside users. Keep your dog under control, especially around livestock, and obey local bylaws and other dog control notices.

Car Parking

Many of the car parks suggested are public, but occasionally you may find you have to park on the roadside or in a lay-by. Please be considerate when you leave your car, ensuring that access roads or gates are not blocked and that other vehicles can pass safely. Remember that pub car parks are private and should not be used unless you have the owner's permission.

An Invigorating Trundle Around Strumble

A walk in some of the wildest countryside of the Pembrokeshire coast.

•DISTANCE•	8 miles (12.9km)
•MINIMUM TIME•	3hrs 30min
•ASCENT / GRADIENT•	920ft (280m) ▲▲▲
•LEVEL OF DIFFICULTY•	👫 👫 👫
•PATHS•	Coast path, grassy, sometimes muddy tracks, rocky paths, 21 stiles
•LANDSCAPE•	Rugged headland, secluded coves and rocky tor
•SUGGESTED MAP•	aqua3 OS Explorer OL35 North Pembrokeshire
•START / FINISH•	Grid reference: SM 894411
•DOG FRIENDLINESS•	Care needed near livestock
•PARKING•	Car park by Strumble Head Lighthouse
•PUBLIC TOILETS•	None on route

BACKGROUND TO THE WALK

This is my favourite stretch of the Pembrokeshire coast, although at times it feels like 'coast path meets the Himalayas', as the narrow ribbon of trail climbs and drops at regular intervals throughout. This is the real wild side of Pembrokeshire.

High Cliffs

The headland cliffs tower above the pounding Atlantic surf, the path cuts an airy, at times precarious, line across their tops and the sky is alive with the sound of seabirds. Atlantic grey seals, porpoises and even dolphins are regularly spotted in the turbulent waters. Garn Fawr, a formidable rocky tor that lords high above the whole peninsula, brings a touch of hill walking to the experience, and the shapely lighthouse flashes a constant reminder of just how treacherous these spectacular waters can be.

Beacon of Light

Built in 1908 to help protect the ferries that run between Fishguard and Ireland, the Strumble Head Lighthouse guards a hazardous stretch of coast that wrecked at least 60 ships in the 19th century alone. The revolving lights, which flash four times every 15 seconds, were originally controlled by a massive clockwork system that needed rewinding every 12 hours. This was replaced in 1965 by an electrically powered system and the lighthouse was then converted to unstaffed operation in 1980. It's possible to cross the daunting narrow chasm that separates Ynys Meicel (St Michael's Island), where the lighthouse stands, from the mainland by a rickety bridge.

Atlantic Grey Seals

This is one of the best walks in Pembrokeshire to spot these lumbering marine giants that reach over 8ft (2.4m) in length and can weigh as much as 770lbs (350kg). They are usually seen bobbing up and down (bottling) in the water just off the coast, but in autumn when the females give birth to a single pup, they often haul up on to inaccessible beaches where the young are suckled on milk with an incredibly high fat content. The pups shed their white coat after around three weeks, when they are then weaned and taught to swim before being abandoned. The males are usually bigger than the females, with a darker coat and a much more pronounced 'Roman' nose. The best places to see seals on this walk are the bays of Pwll Bach and Pwlluog, near the start.

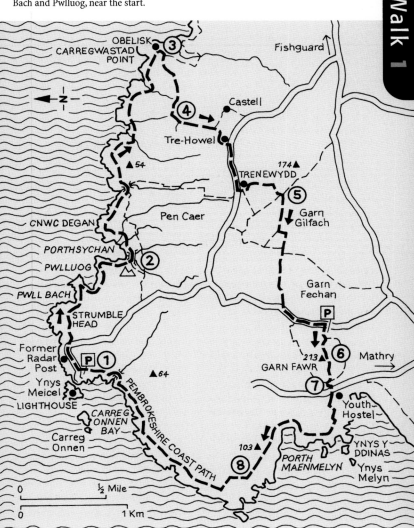

Walk 1 Directions

① Walk back up the road and cross a stile on the left on to the coast path. Pass above the bays of **Pwll** **Bach** and **Pwlluog**, then drop steeply to a footbridge behind the pebble beach of **Porthsychan**.

② Follow the coast path waymarkers around **Cnwc Degan**

WHILE YOU'RE THERE ⓘ

At Carregwastad Point is a stone **obelisk** that marks the spot of the last hostile invasion of Britain. On 22 February 1797, a small French force known as the Legion Noire came ashore and set up camp at Tre-Howel, a local farm. The invaders were quick to take advantage of a huge haul of liquor that had been salvaged from a recent wreck and, subsequently unfit to fight, were forced to surrender within two days.

---

and down to another bridge, where a couple of footpaths lead away from the coast. Continue along the coast, passing a cottage on the right and climbing and dropping a couple of times, before you reach the obelisk at **Carregwastad Point**.

③ Follow the track inland and cross a stile on to a track, where you turn right, away from the coast path. Continue with the path up through the gorse to a wall, then turn right on to a good track. Take this through a succession of gates and around a left-hand bend.

④ Ignore a track to the right and continue up the cattle track to the farmyard where you swing right and then left, after the buildings, to the road. Turn right and follow the road past a large house to a waymarked bridleway on the left.

WHAT TO LOOK FOR ⓘ

The small hut beneath the car park at the start was a World War Two **radar post** which has been converted into a bird observatory. This is one of the best ornithology spots in the country, particularly well known for spotting **migratory birds** leaving in autumn and arriving in the spring. As well as obvious seabirds, look out for early swallows and swifts, also large numbers of warblers and other small migrants.

Pass **Trenewydd** and go through a gate on to a green lane. Follow this up to another gate and on to open ground.

⑤ Turn right here and follow the wall to yet another gate. This leads to a walled track which you follow to the road. Turn left and climb up to the car park beneath **Garn Fawr**. Turn right, on to a hedged track, and follow this up, through a gap in the wall, and over rocks to the trig point.

WHERE TO EAT AND DRINK ⓘ

The one down side about walking in such a wild spot is the lack of facilities. There is occasionally an **ice-cream van** in the car park at the start. Failing that, the best place for food and drink is the **Farmers Arms** in Mathry, further south, or head east towards **Fishguard**, where there's plenty of choice.

---

⑥ Climb down and cross the saddle between this tor and the other, slightly lower, one to the south. From here head west towards an even lower outcrop and pass it on the left. This becomes a clear path that leads down to a stile. Cross this and turn left, then right on to a drive that leads to the road.

⑦ Walk straight across and on to the coast path. Bear right and cross a stile to drop down towards **Ynys y Ddinas**, the small island ahead. Navigation is easy as you follow the coast path north, over **Porth Maenmelyn** and up to a cairn.

⑧ Continue along the coast, towards the lighthouse, until you drop to a footbridge above **Carreg Onnen Bay**. Cross a stile into a field, then another back on to the coast path and return to the car park.

A Rocky Ramble Around the Head

An easy stroll around the dramatic cliffs of one of mainland Britain's most westerly points.

•DISTANCE•	3½ miles (5.7km)
•MINIMUM TIME•	2hrs
•ASCENT / GRADIENT•	425ft (130m) ▲ ▲ ▲
•LEVEL OF DIFFICULTY•	🚶🚶 🚶 🚶
•PATHS•	Coast path, clear paths across heathland, 2 stiles
•LANDSCAPE•	Dramatic cliffs, heather- and gorse-covered hillsides
•SUGGESTED MAP•	aqua3 OS Explorer OL35 North Pembrokeshire
•START / FINISH•	Grid reference: SM 734271
•DOG FRIENDLINESS•	Care needed near livestock
•PARKING•	Whitesands Beach
•PUBLIC TOILETS•	At start

BACKGROUND TO THE WALK

Steeped in legend, peppered with the evidence of civilisations past, and scenically stunning, it would be difficult to imagine a more atmospheric place than St David's Head. For full effect, visit at sunset and watch the sky turn red over the scattered islets of the Bishops and Clerks.

St David's Head

Carn Llidi, a towering monolith of ancient rock that has all the attributes of a full-blown mountain, yet stands only 594ft (181m) above sea level, dominates the headland. Its heather- and gorse-covered flanks are alive with small heathland birds, which chatter from the swaying ferns and dart for cover in the hidden crannies of dry-stone walls.

The coast, when you meet it, is at its intricate finest; a succession of narrow zawns (clefts), broken up by stubborn headlands that thrust defiantly into the ever-present swells. The Head itself is magnificent and a few minutes spent exploring will quickly uncover a series of rocky terraces that offer shelter from the wind and stunning views over the ocean to Ramsey Island and the Bishops and Clerks.

The Warrior's Dyke

Despite its hostile demeanour, St David's Head was once home to a thriving Iron-Age community who lived in huts and kept their stock in a field system, the remains of which are still visible. The headland, naturally guarded by the ocean on three sides, was also defended by the Clawydd-y-Milwry (the Warrior's Dyke) at its eastern edge. The dyke is actually formed by three ditches and two ramparts that cut across the neck of the headland. The main bastion, a dry-stone wall that would have once stood around 15ft (4.6m) tall, is still easily visible as a linear pile of stones and rocks. Within the fort there are a number of standing stones, stone circles and the remains of basic huts. The defences are thought to have been built around AD 100.

Burial Chambers

At least 3,000 years older, but well worth seeking out, is Coetan Arthur, a neolithic quoit, or burial chamber, which stands directly above a narrow zawn, bounded on its eastern walls by the red-coloured crags of Craig Coetan, a popular climbing venue. Coetan Arthur consists of a 12ft (3.7m) long capstone, propped up on a smaller rock. The quoit would have originally been covered with earth to form a mound, but this has long since been eroded away. There is evidence of several more burial chambers near the summit of Carn Llidi. Happily both the headland and Carn Llidi are in the care of the National Trust, and you are free to wander at will to investigate these fascinating sites, although you should bear in mind that they are Scheduled Ancient Monuments and protected by law.

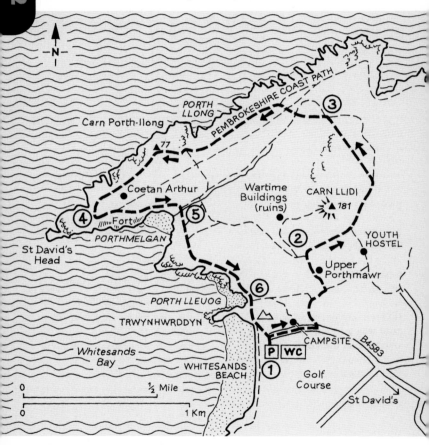

Walk 2 Directions

① From **Whitesands Beach** head back up the road, pass the **campsite**, and a track on the left, and then take the second track on the left. Bear right where it splits

and continue around a left-hand bend to walk up to the buildings. Keep left to walk between the houses, then carry on to a gate.

② Turn right on to the open heathland and follow the footpath along the wall beneath **Carn Llidi**.

Walk 2

Pass the track that drops to the youth hostel on the right and continue around to where the path splits. Take the higher track and keep going in the same direction until, at the corner of a wall, a clear track runs diagonally left towards the coast.

③ Follow this to the coast path and turn left to hug the cliff tops. At **Porth Llong**, the path bears right to climb to a cairn. The headland is a labyrinth of paths and tracks, but for maximum enjoyment try to stick as close to the cliff tops as possible as you round a number of narrow zawns. The official coast path doesn't go as far as the tip of the peninsula, but plenty of other tracks do, so follow one as far as you wish.

④ From the tip, turn left and make your way through the rocky outcrops on the southern side of the headland. As you approach **Porthmelgan** you'll pick up an obvious path that traverses the steep hillside down into a valley, which shelters a small stream.

⑤ Cross the stream and climb up the steps on the other side. Continue to a kissing gate where the National Trust land ends and maintain your direction. Pass above **Porth Lleuog** and the distinctive rocky promontory of **Trwynhwrddyn**, which is worth a visit in its own right.

⑥ The path then drops steeply down to the road at the entrance to **Whitesands Beach**.

Walk 3

Pounding the Sound with a Hermit Monk

Along the shores of Ramsey Sound with great views and excellent wildlife-spotting opportunities.

•DISTANCE•	3½ miles (5.7km)
•MINIMUM TIME•	2hrs
•ASCENT / GRADIENT•	197ft (60m) ▲ ▲ ▲
•LEVEL OF DIFFICULTY•	🚶 🚶 🚶
•PATHS•	Coast path and easy farmland tracks, 5 stiles
•LANDSCAPE•	Undulating coast, dramatic views to Ramsey Island
•SUGGESTED MAP•	aqua3 OS Explorer OL35 North Pembrokeshire
•START / FINISH•	Grid reference: SM 724252
•DOG FRIENDLINESS•	One dog-proof stile and farmyard
•PARKING•	Car park above lifeboat station at St Justinian's
•PUBLIC TOILETS•	Nearest at Porth Clais or Whitesands

BACKGROUND TO THE WALK

This is one of the easiest walks, but it's also one of the most rewarding, with drop-dead gorgeous coastal scenery and plenty of chances to spot some of Pembrokeshire's varied wildlife. On a calm summer's day, the bobbing boats in Ramsey Sound display the kind of tranquillity you'd usually associate with a Greek island. See it on a rough day, with a spring tide running, and the frothing, seething currents that whip through the narrow channel are frightening to say the least. If the views aren't enough, a keen eye and a handy pair of binoculars may well produce sightings of seals, porpoises, dolphins, choughs and even peregrine falcons.

St Justinian

St Justinian was a hermit from Brittany who became the abbot of St David's Cathedral and acted as St David's confessor. Disillusioned with the lethargic attitude of the monks, he absconded to Ramsey Island to establish a more spiritual community. Some of his more loyal monks travelled with him, but eventually even they became fed up with his strict regimes and chopped off his head. It is said he walked back across Ramsey Sound carrying it in his arms.

His remains were buried in the small chapel on the hillside overlooking the sound, which bears his name. Later St David took them to his own church. St Justinian is revered as a martyr, his assassins are thought to have been under demonic influence, and his life is celebrated on December 5th, each year.

Ramsey Island

Less than 2 miles (3.2km) long and 446ft (136m) high at its tallest point, Ramsey Island is a lumbering humpback ridge separated from the St David's coast by a narrow sound. Known in Welsh as Ynys Ddewi – St David's Isle – this is the place where, legend suggests, St David met St Patrick.

It's a haven for wildlife and has belonged to the RSPB as a nature reserve since 1992. The eastern coast looks pretty tame, but the western seaboard boasts some of Pembrokeshire's tallest and most impressive cliffs, punctuated with sea caves and rock arches that are the breeding grounds of the area's largest seal colony. At its narrowest point, a string of jagged rocks protrude into the sound. These are known as The Bitches and they make a terrifying spectacle indeed. Tides gush through the rocks at speeds of up to 8 knots, creating a scene that resembles a mountain river in spate. The resultant waves and eddies make an extreme salt-water playground for white-water kayakers. Looking slightly out of place against the salty ocean backdrop, the island is populated by a herd of red deer.

Harbour Porpoises

Ramsey Sound is one the best places to catch a glimpse of Pembrokeshire's shyest marine mammals, harbour porpoises. Resembling dolphins, though never more than 7ft (2.1m) in length, small schools of these tiny cetaceans crop up all around the coast, but are frequently seen feeding in the currents at either end of the sound. Unlike dolphins, they seldom leap from the water, but their arched backs and small dorsal fins are easy to spot as they surface for air. Choose a day when the water is fairly flat, then scan the ocean from a promontory like Pen Dal-aderyn with a pair of binoculars. Once you spot one, you should find it easy to see others.

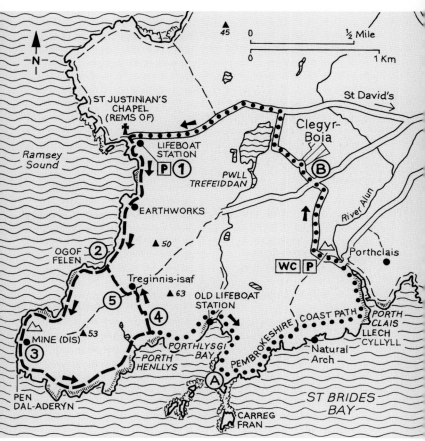

Walk 3

Walk 3 Directions

① Walk down to the lifeboat station and turn left on to the coast path, above the steps. Follow this, passing above a number of lofty, grassy promontories that make great picnic spots. After ½ mile (800m), look out for the traces of Iron-Age earthworks on the left.

> ### WHAT TO LOOK FOR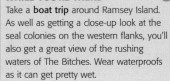
> Take a second look at any of the small crows you see as you follow this stretch of coast path. What appears at first glance to be a jackdaw is probably sporting a sharp red bill and bright red legs and is one of Britain's rarest crows, the **chough**. These small birds are incredibly common in Pembrokeshire, however, where they nest on ledges and feed mainly on insects.

② Pass a gate and a track on your left – this is your return route – and swing around to the west above **Ogof Felen**. This is a good seal pup beach in autumn. The trail climbs slightly and then drops steeply to a ruined copper mine, directly opposite **The Bitches**.

③ Continue easily to **Pen Dal-aderyn** and then swing eastwards to enter **St Brides Bay**. The path climbs above some magnificent cliffs and passes between a few rocky outcrops before veering north above the broad bay of **Porth Henllys**. Drop down into a shallow valley until you come to a fingerpost at a junction of paths.

> ### WHILE YOU'RE THERE ⓘ
> Take a **boat trip** around Ramsey Island. As well as getting a close-up look at the seal colonies on the western flanks, you'll also get a great view of the rushing waters of The Bitches. Wear waterproofs as it can get pretty wet.

④ Turn left and cross a stile on the right, into a field. Turn left to follow the track along the wall to another gate, where you enter a courtyard. Keep left here and pass a barn on the left. When the track opens out into a field, keep right to pass through a gate and on to a waymarked track.

> ### WHERE TO EAT AND DRINK ⓘ
> There are plenty of options in St David's, but the **Low Pressure Café** in the High Street is probably the most popular, especially with surfers, climbers and walkers. It's inexpensive and does great sandwiches and cakes. For pub food and a drink, the **Farmers Arms** in Goat Street, has got to be a favourite (▶ Where To Eat and Drink, Walk 6).

⑤ Follow this waymarked track down between dry-stone walls to reach another gate, which leads back out on to the coast path. Turn right and retrace your outward route along the grassy clifftop path back to **St Justinian's**.

Ramsey Sound to Porth Clais

Double the coast path mileage in exchange for a short road section or, in the summer, take the bus.

See map and information panel for Walk 3

•DISTANCE•	7 miles (11.3km)
•MINIMUM TIME•	3hrs
•ASCENT / GRADIENT•	425ft (130m) ▲▲ ▲ ▲
•LEVEL OF DIFFICULTY•	🚶🚶 🚶🚶 🚶🚶

Walk 4 Directions (Walk 3 option)

For most of the year, this extended walk starts at St Justinian's and you will need to follow the quiet lanes from Porth Clais to finish. In summer, however, it's possible to begin in St David's and take the Celtic Coaster hourly bus service to St Justinian's, then catch it back again from Porth Clais at the end.

Whichever way you chose, follow Walk 3 to Point ④ and stay on the coast path to climb up out of the dip. This leads around **Maen Llwydwyn** and down to **Porthlysgi Bay**. The building on the left as you descend is the original St David's lifeboat station, replaced by the one you passed at St Justinian's. A permissive path runs inland from here, but you need to climb back up, behind the beach, and on to the cliff tops (Point ④) near the rocky island of **Carreg Fran**.

The gradient eases again and the path now cruises comfortably along a wonderful section of coast, studded with rock arches and caves. At **Llech Cyllyll**, turn back inland to drop down into the deeply cloven inlet of **Porth Clais**. The harbour was built in the 12th century and was once the main port for St David's, used for importing coal and timber among other things. The main car park is on the site of the now defunct St David's gasworks. These in turn had been built over the site of a spring, said to be the place that St David was baptised. Porth Clais is also purported to be the landing place of the legendary magic boar, Twrch Trywyth, after he swam from Ireland to confront King Arthur.

Turn left on to the road and climb steeply past the car park. Continue easily to a crossroads and keep straight ahead to pass **Clegyr-Boia** (Point ⑧) and the small lake of **Pwll Trefeiddan**, a popular stop-over for migrating waterfowl. Turn left at the T-junction and follow the road back to **St Justinian's**.

WHAT TO LOOK FOR ⓘ

St David's lifeboat station was built in 1911 and replaced the original station situated in Porthlysgi Bay. The current boat is called the *Garside* and was commissioned on 25 May, 1988. The station was used to make the ITV drama series, *Lifeboat*, in the early 1990s when Ramsey Island took on the name of Pendragon Island.

Walk 5

The Northern Reaches of St Brides Bay

A linear jaunt along a fine stretch of coast.

•DISTANCE•	9 miles (14.5km)
•MINIMUM TIME•	4hrs
•ASCENT / GRADIENT•	1,280ft (390m) ▲▲▲
•LEVEL OF DIFFICULTY•	🚶🚶 🚶🚶 🚶
•PATHS•	Coast path, 14 stiles
•LANDSCAPE•	High cliffs and sheltered coves
•SUGGESTED MAP•	aqua3 OS Explorer OL35 North Pembrokeshire
•START•	Grid reference: SM 757252
•FINISH•	Grid reference: SM 847223
•DOG FRIENDLINESS•	Care needed near cliff edges
•PARKING•	Pay-and-display car park in St David's
•PUBLIC TOILETS•	By tourist information centre at start and at Solva

Walk 5 Directions

When it comes to coast paths, circular walks are a means to an end, but connoisseurs will always prefer the simplicity of a linear route, especially as there's no need to dilute the quality of the coastal section with often less interesting terrain. The key to success is public transport and fortunately there are a few stretches of the Pembrokeshire Coast Path that link well with buses to allow some of the finest walks to be completed without compromise. This section, along the northern reaches of St Brides Bay, is one the best.

Turn left out of the car park in **St David's** and walk down the road towards **Caerfai Bay**. You'll meet the coast path on the left-hand side of a small car park. Follow it down, ignoring a right turn to the beach, and bear south to round a broad promontory, tipped with a rocky bluff. The path swings left and drops down to **Caer Bwdy**, where you'll pass a ruined mill on the left. Climb back up on to the cliff tops to continue above **Carreg y Barcud** and around another inlet. The next section slips by easily, above a series of caves and arches, before you drop steeply down to **Porth y Rhaw**.

Climb out again and enjoy huge views over more cliffs and bluffs. One mile (1.6km) after Porth y Rhaw, you'll be drawn back inland as the path dips into the sharp gash of **Solva**. Go through a gate and follow the field edge down to

Walk 5

another gate, on the right. This leads on to a narrow track. Follow this past some houses, then keep ahead to join the path again. Drop down a path on the right and follow the slipway along the side of the harbour. Like Porth Clais, Solva was once a busy shipping centre and, during the 19th century, it was even used as an embarkation point for voyages to America.

WHERE TO EAT AND DRINK   ⓘ

There's plenty of choice of pubs and tea rooms in **St David's** and **Solva**. There's also a small **café** at Newgale, and the **Duke of Edinburgh** pub does reasonable food.

At the head of the inlet, cross the bridge by the **Harbour Inn** and turn right to walk along the other bank, past a cluster of lime kilns. The path then bears left, steeply up on to the ridge of **Gribin**. The names Gribin or Cribin, literally translate to ridge. At the seaward end you'll pass the banks of an Iron-Age settlement before dropping steeply down steps to a footbridge in the valley below. Cross the pebbles at the back of the beach and climb steeply up on to the headland of **Penrhyn**. Don't be drawn right here but keep straight ahead to rejoin the cliff edge, a short distance further on.

The path continues to climb steadily from this point, passing above a few beautiful beaches before dropping slightly above the pronounced rocky peninsula of **Dinas Fawr**. An airy scramble along its back makes a great excursion if time allows. Continue easily above **Stacen y Brenhin** and then drop again into a deep valley by **Porthmynawyd**. Cross a footbridge and climb the steps back on to the cliff tops once more.

The wide sweeping sands of Newgale are now visible ahead and, as you are drawn back inland at **Cwm-bach**, you should be able to see if the tide is low enough to allow you to finish the walk on the beach itself or whether you'll need to climb back up on to the coast path from **Cwm Mawr**.

Climb away from Cwm-bach and then, almost immediately, drop into Cwm Mawr. The beach is accessed by a short scramble down rocks on the right. If the tide's out, continue easily along the beach, past a number of huge caves, to **Newgale**. Once on **Newgale Beach**, keep the cliffs to your left and walk up to the huge pebble bank above. Scale this and cross behind the small stream to gain the road.

If the tide's too high, climb away from Cwm Mawr and continue along the coast path, with fantastic views west along the coast. This leads out on to the road at **Newgale**, where you turn right to drop to the village.

WHAT TO LOOK FOR   ⓘ

The towering cliffs that make up most of this walk provide perfect roosts and nesting ledges for one of Britain's most spectacular birds, the **peregrine falcon**. These raptors are capable of diving at over 200mph (320kph), and are easily distinguished from kestrels as they are considerably stockier with a short tail and slate grey uppers. Spring and summer tend to be the best time to see them, as the adult birds are busy finding food for their brood, which when fledged, tend to advertise their spectacular flight practice with a high-pitched *kek-kek-kek* call.

Walk 6

A Pilgrimage Around St Non's Bay

Easy walking around the wonderful coastline that gave birth to the patron saint.

•DISTANCE•	3½ miles (5.7km)
•MINIMUM TIME•	1hr 30min
•ASCENT / GRADIENT•	262ft (80m) ▲ ▲ ▲
•LEVEL OF DIFFICULTY•	𝟰𝟰 𝟰𝟰 𝟰𝟰
•PATHS•	Coast path and clear footpaths over farmland, 6 stiles
•LANDSCAPE•	Leafy countryside and dramatic cliffs
•SUGGESTED MAP•	aqua3 OS Explorer OL35 North Pembrokeshire
•START / FINISH•	Grid reference: SM 757252
•DOG FRIENDLINESS•	On lead around St Non's Chapel and well
•PARKING•	Pay-and-display car park in St David's
•PUBLIC TOILETS•	Next to tourist information centre

BACKGROUND TO THE WALK

This walk makes a great evening stroll. The paths that lead from the city are pleasant and easy to follow but as always they're quickly forgotten as you step out into the more glamorous surroundings of the coast. The all-too-short section of towering buttresses and jagged islets leads easily to a spot that can claim to be the very heart of spiritual Wales – the birthplace of St David. The serenity of the location soothes the mind in readiness for the short jaunt back to the compact little city he founded.

Patron Saint
Considering the immense influence he has had on Welsh culture, little is known about the patron saint himself. His mother is said to be St Non, derived from Nun or Nonita, who was married to a local chieftain called Sant. They settled somewhere near Trwyn Cynddeiriog, the rocky bluff that forms the western walls of the bay named after her.

Calming Influence
Legend suggests that David was born around AD 500, in the place where the ruined chapel stands today. Although a fierce storm raged throughout his birth, a calm light was said to have lit the scene. By the morning, a fresh spring had erupted near by, becoming the Holy Well of St Non and visited on this walk. St David went on to be baptised by St Elvis at Porthclais, in water from another miraculous spring.

Man With a Mission
Judging from his parentage, David would have been well educated and it is believed that he undertook a number of religious odysseys, including one to Jerusalem, before he finally returned to his birthplace around AD 550. He then founded a church and monastery at Glyn Rhosyn, on the banks of the River Alun, on the site of the present cathedral, where he set about trying to spread the Christian word to the, mainly pagan, Celts before his death in 589.

St David's Day is celebrated on 1 March every year and St Non, who saw out her life in Brittany, is remembered on the day after.

St David's City
St David's is little more than a pretty village, though it boasts the title 'city' due to its magnificent cathedral. It's a wonderful place and doesn't seem any the worse for the amount of tourism that it attracts. Known as Tyddewi – David's House – in Welsh, the city grew as a result of its coastal position at the western extreme of the British mainland. It would have been linked easily by sea with Ireland and Cornwall. As well as the cathedral and the ruins of the Bishop's Palace, it houses a plethora of gift shops and the National Park information centre, close to the car park, is one of the finest in the country.

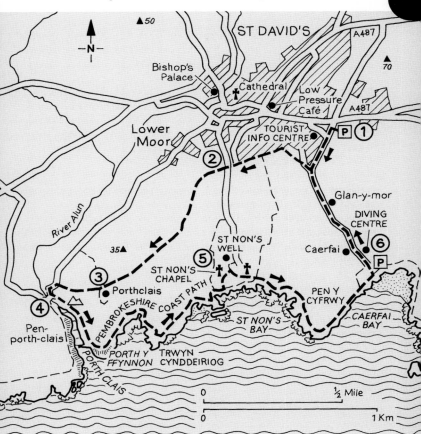

Walk 6 Directions

① Turn left out of the car park in St David's and walk down the road, as if you were heading for **Caerfai Bay**. As the houses thin out, you'll see a turning on the right that leads to more dwellings. Take this and then turn left on to a waymarked bridleway. Follow this bridleway between hedges, past the end of a road and on to a junction with another road.

Walk 6

② Walk straight across and take the waymarked path down a pleasant track to a stile. Cross and keep to the left of the field to another stile, where you keep straight ahead again. This leads to a farmyard, which is also a caravan park.

WHERE TO EAT AND DRINK

Apart from the possibility of an **ice-cream van** in the car park at Porth Clais, the best bet for refreshment is St David's where there's plenty of choice. A favourite pub is the **Farmers Arms** on Goat Street, which has a good garden and serves up all the usual pub fare. For non-alcoholic refreshment, try the excellent **Low Pressure Café** (► Where to Eat and Drink, Walk 3).

③ Turn right and keep the hedge on your right, where the drive swings off to the left. Continue across this field and at the end drop down between gorse bushes to the road at **Porth Clais**. Turn left to the bottom of the valley and then, before crossing the bridge, turn left on to the coast path.

④ Climb up steeply on to the cliff tops and bear around to the left to walk towards **Porth y Ffynnon**. The next small headland is **Trwyn Cynddeiriog**, where there's a lovely grassy platform above the cliffs if you fancy a rest. Continue walking into **St Non's Bay** and look for a footpath on the left that leads to the ruined chapel.

⑤ From the chapel, head up to a gate that leads to **St Non's Well** and, from there, follow the path beneath the new chapel and back out on to the coast path. Turn left to climb easily on to **Pen y Cyfrwy**, continue around this and drop down towards **Caerfai Bay**.

⑥ You'll eventually come out beneath the Caerfai Bay car park where you turn left on to the road. Follow this past the **Diving Centre** to **St David's** and the start of the walk.

WHILE YOU'RE THERE

St David's Cathedral is both architecturally stunning and spiritually moving. In 1120 Pope Calixtus II decreed that two pilgrimages to St David's were the equivalent of one to Rome – an honour indeed. The cathedral and the nearby Bishop's Palace play host to a series of classical concerts every summer.

WHAT TO LOOK FOR

Shortly after the stiff climb out of Porth Clais, you'll round **Trwyn Cynddeiriog**, the headland that divides Porth y Ffynnon from St Non's Bay. This is where St Non and Sant, St David's parents, were said to have lived. A short distance further along the coast path, at the head of the bay, you'll see a footpath on the left that leads to the ruined **chapel**. This is thought to have been built in the 13th century on the spot where St David was born. A path then leads to a gate, behind which you'll see **St Non's Well** and a grotto. Further up the hill is the newer chapel, dedicated to Our Lady and St Non. This was actually built in the 1930s using stone from other principle local evangelical sites, including the original chapel.

Broad Haven and the Haroldston Woods

A winding path through mixed woodland and an easy stroll above the Haroldston cliffs.

•DISTANCE•	3½ miles (5.7km)
•MINIMUM TIME•	1hr 30min
•ASCENT / GRADIENT•	290ft (88m) ▲ ▲ ▲
•LEVEL OF DIFFICULTY•	🚶 🚶 🚶
•PATHS•	Woodland trail, country lanes and coast path, 1 stile
•LANDSCAPE•	Mixed woodland and lofty cliffs above broad beach
•SUGGESTED MAP•	aqua3 OS Explorer OL36 South Pembrokeshire
•START / FINISH•	Grid reference: SM 863140
•DOG FRIENDLINESS•	Poop scoop around car park and beach
•PARKING•	Car park by tourist information centre in Broad Haven
•PUBLIC TOILETS•	Between car park and beach

BACKGROUND TO THE WALK

Woodland walking is something of a rarity along the Pembrokeshire Coast Path, so this short stretch of permissive path, which sneaks through a narrow strip of woodland separating Broad Haven from Haroldston, makes a refreshing diversion from the usual salty air and the cries of the seabirds. This is the easiest of the Pembrokeshire walks in the book, with an almost billiard table-level section of coast path, some of which has been surfaced for access by wheelchair users. The artificial path, however, takes nothing away from the quality of the scenery, which is magnificent.

Eroding Cliffs

The cliffs here are of softer shales and millstone grit making them prone to erosion and subsidence, as you'll witness firsthand along the way. Amazingly, this whole stretch of coast sits on top of huge coal reserves, but the last colliery, which was situated further north in Nolton Haven, actually closed down in the early 1900s. As you progress south you'll pass the crumpled remains of an Iron-Age fort on Black Point – although this is rapidly becoming separated from the main cliff by a landslide – and also a diminutive standing stone, known as the Harold Stone, which is tucked away in a field on the left as you approach Broad Haven. It's said to mark the spot where Harold, the Earl of Wessex, defeated the Welsh in the 11th century, but it's actually more likely to be Bronze Age.

Coastal Resort

Broad Haven is about as close as you'll get to a traditional seaside resort in North Pembrokeshire. The town's popularity as a holiday destination blossomed in the early 1800s, but recent years have seen an acceleration in development that has resulted in almost wall-to-wall caravan parks and a significant rise in the number of residential properties. The beach is beautiful, with gently sloping sands encased in brooding dark cliffs. As well as the usual selection of family holiday-makers, it's a popular place with windsurfers. This is due partly to a shop and rental centre behind the beach, and because the prevalent south westerlies that blow across and onshore from the left make it a safe but fun place to play in the sometimes sizeable surf.

Rock Formations

At low tide it's possible to walk south along the beach to the charming village of Little Haven. A walk northwards will reveal some fascinating rock formations beneath the headland. These include Den's Door, an impressive double arch in a rugged sea stack; the Sleek Stone, a humpbacked rock forced into its contorted position by a geological fault; and Shag Rock and Emmet Rock. Contorted layers of rock are also clearly visible in the main cliffs.

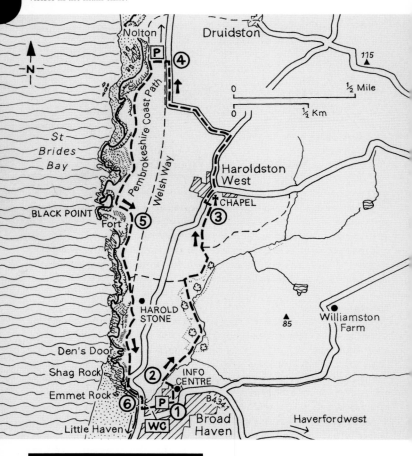

Walk 7 Directions

① From anywhere in the car park, walk towards the National Park information centre and follow a waymarked path ('Woodland Walk')

that runs between the information centre and the coastguard rescue building. Go right and then left to a bridge. Cross the bridge and continue straight ahead through a kissing gate, with the stream on your left.

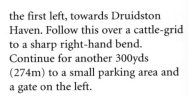

WHERE TO EAT AND DRINK

There's plenty of choice, including pubs, cafés and chip shops in **Broad Haven**, but the top place for atmosphere, food and setting has to be the **Swan** on the tiny harbourside in Little Haven. It's an intimate little pub ideal for lunch, dinner or just a pint on the sea wall (children and dogs not allowed inside).

② Ignore a faint path forking to the right and continue, on a boardwalk, through the wood. After ½ mile (800m) you'll come to a waymarked path on the left; ignore this and keep straight ahead until you arrive at a junction of paths beneath a small **chapel** on your right.

③ Turn left to the road and then right on to it to walk uphill, with the church on your right. Keep ahead at the T-junction, then take

the first left, towards Druidston Haven. Follow this over a cattle-grid to a sharp right-hand bend. Continue for another 300yds (274m) to a small parking area and a gate on the left.

④ Go through this and follow the well-surfaced track down towards the coast. On reaching the cliff tops, bear around to the left and continue past **Black Point**.

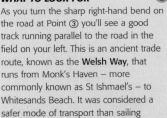

WHAT TO LOOK FOR

As you turn the sharp right-hand bend on the road at Point ③ you'll see a good track running parallel to the road in the field on your left. This is an ancient trade route, known as the **Welsh Way**, that runs from Monk's Haven — more commonly known as St Ishmael's — to Whitesands Beach. It was considered a safer mode of transport than sailing across the troubled waters of the bay.

⑤ After passing the **Harold Stone** on your left, the path starts to drop, generally quite easily but there is one steep step. Follow the path down to meet the road and keep right to drop to the walkway above the beach.

⑥ Cross over the bridge and then, just before the road you are on merges into the main road, turn left on to a tarmac footpath that leads through a green and back to the car park.

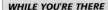

WHILE YOU'RE THERE

A few miles north, in the tiny hamlet of Nolton, there's an excellent, if sometimes rowdy, place called the **Celtic Corner**. Every Wednesday night, during the summer, they hold Welsh nights, a heady mix of Welsh music, traditional food and of course, the odd tipple. Probably not a good idea if you're planning to start early the next day.

Walk 8

Island Views from the Marloes Peninsula

An easy walk around a windswept headland overlooking two offshore islands and a marine nature reserve.

•DISTANCE•	6 miles (9.7km)
•MINIMUM TIME•	2hrs 30min
•ASCENT / GRADIENT•	420ft (128m)
•LEVEL OF DIFFICULTY•	
•PATHS•	Coast path and clear footpaths, short section on tarmac, 10 stiles
•LANDSCAPE•	Rugged cliff tops and beautiful sandy beaches
•SUGGESTED MAP•	aqua3 OS Explorer OL36 South Pembrokeshire
•START / FINISH•	Grid reference: SM 761089
•DOG FRIENDLINESS•	Poop scoop on beaches
•PARKING•	National Trust car park above Martin's Haven, near Marloes village
•PUBLIC TOILETS•	Marloes village

BACKGROUND TO THE WALK

The Marloes Peninsula forms the westernmost tip of the southern shores of St Brides Bay. The paddle-shaped headland is a popular place to walk due to the narrow neck that affords minimum inland walking for maximum time spent on the coast. It is famous for its stunning scenery, which includes two of the Pembrokeshire Coast National Park's finest and least-crowded beaches, some secluded coves that are often inhabited by seals, and wonderfully rugged coastline. There are also fine views over a narrow but turbulent sound to the small islands of Skomer and Skokholm – two significant seabird breeding grounds. The walking is captivating, even by Pembrokeshire standards.

Wildlife Sanctuary
Skomer is the largest of the Pembrokeshire islands and is one of the most significant wildlife habitats in the whole country. The island, separated from the mainland by the rushing waters of Jack Sound, measures approximately 1½ miles (2.4km) from north to south and 2 miles (3.2km) from east to west. It was declared a National Nature Reserve in 1959 and, as well as the protection it receives as part of the National Park, it's also designated as a Site of Special Scientific Interest (SSSI), a Special Protection Area (SPA) and a Geological Conservation Review Site (GCR). Much of the land is a Scheduled Ancient Monument, courtesy of a number of clearly visible Iron-Age settlements and enclosures. If that's not enough of an accolade, the sea that surrounds the island is a Marine Nature Reserve, one of only two in the United Kingdom; the other is Lundy, off the North Devon coast.

Puffins and Shearwaters
The two stars of the Skomer show are the diminutive but colourful puffin and the dowdy and secretive Manx shearwater. Puffins need little introduction; their colourful beaks and

Walk 8

clown-like facial markings put them high on everybody's list of favourite birds. There are around 6,000 nesting pairs on Skomer. They arrive in April and lay a single egg in a burrow. The chick hatches at the end of May and the adult birds spend the next two months ferrying back catches of sand eels for their flightless offspring. After around seven weeks of this lavish attention the chick leaves the nest, usually at night, and makes its way to the sea. Assuming that it learns to look after itself successfully, it will spend the next few years at sea, only returning when it reaches breeding maturity.

Bashful Birds

The mouse-like shearwater is slightly larger than the puffin but it also lays its single egg in a burrow, overlooking the sea. It may not be as obviously endearing as its painted neighbour, especially as most visitors to the island never actually see one, but it's a beautiful and fascinating bird in its own right and there are in fact around 150,000 pairs on Skomer, Skokholm and Middleholm; which amounts to about 60 per cent of the world's total population. The reason they are seldom seen is because they are fairly vulnerable to predators on land so they leave the nest at dawn and spend the whole day at sea, not returning to their burrow until it's almost dark. A careful seawatch at last light may reveal them gathering in huge rafts just offshore or even endless lines of flying birds returning to the island – against the sunset, it's quite a magical sight.

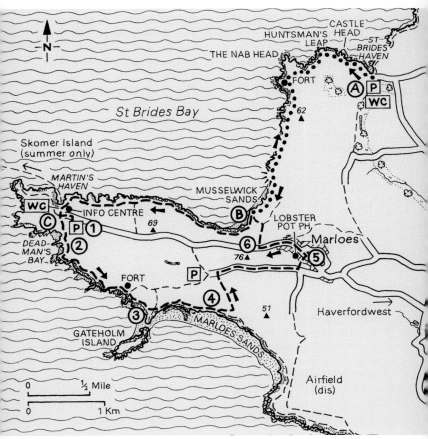

Walk 8

Walk 8 Directions

① From the car park turn left on to the road and walk down to the bottom of the hill. Bear around to the left, then go through the gate straight ahead into the **Deer Park**. Turn left and follow the path along to a stile and out on to the coast.

WHILE YOU'RE THERE ⓘ

If you have a day to spare then **Skomer Island** is well worth a visit. The *Dale Princess*, a 50-seat passenger boat, departs Martin's Haven regularly every morning during summer and returns during the afternoon. As well as the wildlife and the relics of ancient civilisations, there's also some fine walking. Note that dogs are not allowed on the island.

---

② With the sea to your right, continue easily along over **Deadman's Bay** to another stile. The next section cruises along easily, passing the earthworks of an Iron-Age fort on the left and crossing another stile as you approach **Gateholm Island**.

③ It is possible to get across to the island at low tide, but care is needed to scramble over the slippery rocks. To continue the walk, follow the coast path, above the western end of the beautiful **Marloes Sands** until you drop easily to the main beach access path.

④ Turn left and climb up to the road; turn right here. Follow the road along for around ¾ mile (1.2km) to a bridleway on the left. Follow this down and turn left into **Marloes** village.

⑤ Pass the **Lobster Pot** on the left and continue ahead to leave the village. Ignore a few tracks on the right, as the road bends around to the left, and continue out into open countryside where you'll meet a footpath on the right.

⑥ Walk down the edge of the field and bear around to the left to drop back down on to the coast path above **Musselwick Sands**. Turn left and follow the path west for over 1½ miles (2.4km) to **Martin's Haven**. Meet the road and climb past the information centre back to the car park.

WHERE TO EAT AND DRINK ⓘ

The **Lobster Pot** in Marloes is conveniently placed at the halfway point of the walk, but no dogs or muddy boots, please. Alternatively, head for **Dale** or **Little Haven** at the end of the walk (▶ Where To Eat and Drink, Walks 7 and 10) as both offer better options.

WHAT TO LOOK FOR ⓘ

If you're walking along the coast in spring or summer you'll not fail to be impressed by the small white and pink flowers that carpet the cliff tops. These are **sea campion** (white) and **thrift** (pink), both common along the Pembrokeshire coast.

As you approach Musselwick Sands on Walk 9, you should be able to see a small island some 8 miles (12.9km) offshore. This is Grassholm and during the summer months it appears almost pure white. It isn't due to the colour of the rock but 30,000 breeding pairs of **gannets** that return to the island every year. Unlike the puffins and shearwaters of Skomer, the gannets are easily spotted, usually in small flocks, cruising a few hundred yards out looking for fish. If you spot them, watch closely and you'll probably witness their spectacular dive as they fold in their wings and plummet like darts into the water.

St Brides Haven and the Marloes Peninsula

An easy extension of Walk 8, starting at St Brides Haven and following more of the glorious coast path.
See map and information panel for Walk 8

•DISTANCE•	10 miles (16.1km)
•MINIMUM TIME•	4hrs 30min
•ASCENT / GRADIENT•	820ft (250m) ▲ ▲ ▲
•LEVEL OF DIFFICULTY•	🚶 🚶 🚶
•START / FINISH•	Grid Reference: SM 802108
•PARKING•	In front of church in St Brides Haven

Walk 9 Directions (Walk 8 option)

This walk extends the easy saunter around the peninsula described in Walk 8 by starting at St Brides Haven and following the coast path to Musselwick Sands, where the two walks merge. St Brides boasts a sheltered, secluded bay, which makes a great spot for a peaceful afternoon on the beach, and the coast path walking from here to Musselwick is both exceptionally pretty and unusually flat, providing plenty of interest for minimum effort. Although it's possible to make this extension into a true circuit by following footpaths north from Marloes village, the coast path is far more interesting. I'm therefore making no apologies for the out-and-back nature of the extension, which follows one of my favourite sections of coast.

From the church (Point Ⓐ) walk to the head of the inlet and turn left to cross the top of the beach and join the coast path as it climbs up towards **Castle Head**. The path climbs steadily upwards to **Huntsman's Leap**, a narrow cleft in the headland, and then tracks south west towards **The Nab Head** where it finally heads south. Shortly after this, you'll pass the earthworks of an Iron-Age fort.

The next section is straightforward with no navigation to think about. Continue down into a dip and back up some steps to enjoy the views south to Skomer and Grassholm. Eventually, you'll pass above the broad expanse of beach that makes up **Musselwick Sands**. Drop into a steep sided dip and you'll meet a footpath coming in from the left. Here you join Walk 8 at Point Ⓑ.

Stay on the Coast Path to follow the instruction for Point ⑥ westwards to Point Ⓒ, at **Martin's Haven**. At the top of lane, stay on the coast path and pass through the gate in the wall, to follow Points ① to ⑤. These lead you to **Marloes Sands**, through **Marloes** and, on the first part of Point ⑥, back to Point Ⓑ, where you turn right to retrace your steps to **St Brides Haven**.

Walk 10

A Simple Circuit of St Ann's Head

High cliffs and rough seas mark the location of Pembrokeshire's biggest environmental catastrophe.

•DISTANCE•	6½ miles (10.4km)
•MINIMUM TIME•	3hrs
•ASCENT / GRADIENT•	590ft (180m) ▲ ▲ ▲
•LEVEL OF DIFFICULTY•	🚶 🚶 🚶
•PATHS•	Coast path, clear paths across farmland, 20 stiles
•LANDSCAPE•	Dramatic coastline and entrance to Milford Haven
•SUGGESTED MAP•	aqua3 OS Explorer OL36 South Pembrokeshire
•START / FINISH•	Grid reference: SM 811058
•DOG FRIENDLINESS•	Care needed near livestock
•PARKING•	Large car park next to beach in Dale
•PUBLIC TOILETS•	At start

Walk 10 Directions

Leave the car park by the exit at the rear and follow the drive to the road. Turn left and walk to a sharp left turn, by **Dale Castle**, where a footpath leads straight ahead. Follow this up through two fields to a stile that leads on to the coast path above the quiet surfing beach of **Westdale Bay**. Turn left and climb the steps up on to **Great Castle Head**, occupied by an

Iron-Age fort. For the next 2 miles (3.2km), continue along the coast path with the sea to your right and farmland to your left. Despite the spectacular scenery, there are no real drops or climbs and no real opportunities to get lost. Relax and enjoy the ambience until you arrive at the **Coastguard Headquarters** on **St Ann's Head**.

When you meet the road, turn right and walk along the drive, past the lookout tower, to a gate. Here, the coast path veers left and then right, to follow a series of marker posts along a fence towards the lighthouse and a bank of cottages on the right. At the cottages, turn sharp left to cross the green to a track that leads behind a walled enclosure. This then drops to join the coast again above **Mill Bay**, where a notice gives details of the landing of the exiled Henry Tudor, Earl of Richmond, in 1485, on his way to the Battle of Bosworth. Descend to cross the head of the

Walk 10

bay and climb up again to follow field edges around to the beacon on **West Blockhouse Point**. You'll pass a pair of dew ponds and then come to a crossroads, where you keep straight ahead.

The path again swings inland, this time to drop down to the finest of the beaches along this stretch, **Watwick Bay**. Again, climb away from the beach and follow the path, both on cliff tops and field edges, to the beacon on **Watwick Point**. After running along the edge of another two fields, cross a stile and drop to the right to start the descent to **Castlebeach**. Cross the footbridge and climb up steps towards the narrow peninsula of **Dale Point**. As the ground levels, you'll meet a junction of paths where you keep straight ahead to the road. Turn left and follow it down, through woodland, to **Dale** and the car park.

The precarious balance between the region's oil refinery and the fragile ecosystems of some of Britain's finest coastline was destroyed on 15 February 1996, when the *Sea Empress* oil tanker grounded on rocks just off St Ann's Head. The collision wasn't particularly bad and because it had taken place near low-tide, the ship could have been quickly recovered had the right systems been in place. Tragically, the recovery became a comedy of errors. Numerous realistic salvage propositions were refused and, though the fated ship still had working engines, at one stage she was allegedly denied permission to continue into port under her own steam. By the Sunday evening, she was still stranded, having lost only 2,000 tonnes of her cargo. High winds and strong tides continued to batter her against the rocks and finally, six days after she first grounded, she limped into the Haven having spilt at least 72,000 tonnes. The affects were catastrophic; huge oil slicks hit 175 miles (280km) of coastline, including the National Park, 35 Sites of Specific Scientific Interest and a National Marine Nature Reserve. The immediate victims were the birds; 6,900 were recovered either dead or rescued, but it is estimated that over 20,000 died. The species worst hit was a small black duck known as the common scoter. The damage to fish stocks and other marine life, will take years to gauge accurately. The tourist industry was temporarily devastated and the full effect on fishing and related trades won't be known for some time. The port still doesn't have the navigation aids and tug power needed to prevent a similar disaster from occurring.

WHAT TO LOOK FOR   ⓘ

The **blockhouses** and **fort** along this stretch of coast show how much strategic military importance was placed on Milford Haven in the past. West Blockhouse, above Watwick Bay, was built in 1857 for a garrison of 80 men. Dale Fort, now a field study centre and seen towards the end of the walk, was also built in the 1850s and would have been garrisoned by a similar number of men. The beacons that dominate the headlands now are part of a complex series of waymarkers that aid tankers into the Haven.

Two Faces of the Haven

The waters of Milford Haven and the coastline that forms its entrance.

•DISTANCE•	8 miles (12.9km)
•MINIMUM TIME•	3hrs 30min
•ASCENT / GRADIENT•	1,017ft (310m) ▲▲ ▲
•LEVEL OF DIFFICULTY•	🚶 🚶 🚶
•PATHS•	Coast path and easy tracks over agricultural land, short road section, 37 stiles
•LANDSCAPE•	Rugged coastline, magnificent beach and sheltered harbour
•SUGGESTED MAP•	aqua3 OS Explorer OL36 South Pembrokeshire
•START / FINISH•	Grid reference: SM 854031
•DOG FRIENDLINESS•	Care needed near livestock
•PARKING•	Car park at West Angle Bay
•PUBLIC TOILETS•	At start and just off route in Angle village

BACKGROUND TO THE WALK

The narrow finger of land that juts out between Freshwater West and Angle Bay forms the eastern wall of the mouth of Milford Haven. On the northern edge of the peninsula, the waters are passive, lapping against a coastline that's gentle and sloping, but as you round the headland, a radical transformation takes place. Here, the cliffs stand tall and proud, defiantly resisting the full brunt of the considerable Atlantic swells. There are other differences too. While the views along the seaward coast are wild and unspoilt, the inner shores of the Haven reveal the ugly scars of industry. The smoking chimneys of the oil refinery dominate the eastern skyline and the inshore waters are criss-crossed with an unsightly patchwork of jetties.

Challenging Route

The narrow-necked shape of the peninsula lends itself to a challenging circular walk that shows both sides of the coin. The outward leg, as far as the sweeping sands of Freshwater West, is about as tough as coast path walking gets; constantly dipping and climbing on narrow, often quite exposed, paths. The return leg is a little more civilised, tracking easily around the curve of Angle Bay and following field edges back out on to the headland.

Whaling Town

Milford Haven is the name of both a huge natural inlet, once described by Admiral Nelson as 'the finest port in Christendom', and the small town that nestles on its northern shores. Despite the obvious advantages of the sheltered waterways, the Haven saw only limited development until the 20th century. Although there is evidence of earlier settlements and shipping activity, the town, as it is now, and original dock, sprang up in the late 1700s to house a small whaling community that had fled from Nantucket, Massachusetts, during the American War of Independence. Despite interest from the military, which saw the potential for shipbuilding, lack of funding at the time prohibited serious expansion. Various enterprising ideas followed over the ensuing years, but by the end of the 19th century, the whaling had all but declined and the Navy had moved to nearby Pembroke Dock.

Lifelines and Controversy

Large-scale fishing in the rich waters of the Pembrokeshire coast threw the port a lifeline in the early 1900s and then, as this too declined, mainly due to over-fishing and the related smaller catches, energy production took over as the area's main industry. There were once three refineries and a power station at the head of the Haven. One of the refineries has now closed and the power station is being dismantled after bowing to considerable public pressure against its plan to burn Orimulsion, a controversial fuel with a contested safety record, instead of oil.

Walk 11

Walk 11 Directions

① Facing the sea, walk left out of the car park and pass between the café and the public conveniences to a waymarked stile. Follow the field edge along, crossing further stiles to a narrow, hedged track that leads to a set of stone steps.

② Follow a good track for a few paces and then fork right to drop towards the ruined **tower** on the headland. Continue back up, cross more stiles and then go down to a footbridge. Climb up from this and pass **Sheep Island** on your right.

WHAT TO LOOK FOR
Milford Haven's potential vulnerability to invasion has led to considerable defences being constructed around its entrance. The stone **blockhouse** on Thorn Island, now a hotel, is testament to this, as are the other fortifications on St Ann's Head (► Walk 10).

---

③ Continue along the coast, dropping steeply into a succession of valleys and climbing back up each time. As you reach the northern end of **Freshwater West**, keep your eye open for a footpath waymarker to the left.

④ Cross a stile and walk up the floor of the valley, swinging left to a stile at the top. Cross the next field, and another stile, and continue to the road (**B4320**). Turn left on to the road and walk past a cluster of houses to a right-hand turn. Follow this down to the coast, turn left on to the coast path and merge on to a drive.

⑤ Take the drive to a footpath sign on the right. If the tide is low, you can cross the estuary here and

continue along the bank of pebbles to the road on the other side. If it's not, carry on along the road into **Angle** village and bear right by the church to follow a dirt track along the other side.

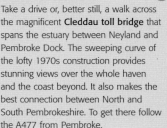

WHILE YOU'RE THERE
Take a drive or, better still, a walk across the magnificent **Cleddau toll bridge** that spans the estuary between Neyland and Pembroke Dock. The sweeping curve of the lofty 1970s construction provides stunning views over the whole haven and the coast beyond. It also makes the best connection between North and South Pembrokeshire. To get there follow the A477 from Pembroke.

---

⑥ Continue around, pass the **Old Point House Inn** on your left and follow field edges to the gravel turning point above the **lifeboat station** on your right. Keep straight ahead, over a stile, and follow the bottom of the field system into a wooded area.

⑦ You'll join a broad track that runs around **Chapel Bay cottages** and fort. Keep right, to cross a stile and follow the narrow path back above the coast. This rounds the headland by **Thorn Island**.

⑧ As you descend into **West Angle Bay**, the path diverts briefly into a field to avoid a landslide. Continue downwards and bear right on to a drive that drops you back to the car park.

WHERE TO EAT AND DRINK
The **Hibernia Inn** in Angle village is conveniently placed for lunch or a drink, but there's also the **Wavecrest Café**, at the start of the walk, and the stunningly positioned **Old Point House Inn**, as you climb above Angle Bay and back out on to the headland.

Beaches and Lakes at Stackpole

An undemanding tour of the cliff tops, beaches and lakes at the southernmost point of the Pembrokeshire Coast National Park.

•DISTANCE•	6 miles (9.7km)
•MINIMUM TIME•	2hrs 30min
•ASCENT / GRADIENT•	390ft (119m) ▲ △ △
•LEVEL OF DIFFICULTY•	🚶🚶 🚶🚶 🚶🚶
•PATHS•	Easy coast path, quiet lanes and well trodden waterside walkways, 1 stile
•LANDSCAPE•	Magnificent limestone headlands, secluded beaches and tranquil waterways
•SUGGESTED MAP•	aqua3 OS Explorer OL36 South Pembrokeshire
•START / FINISH•	Grid reference: SR 976938
•DOG FRIENDLINESS•	Care needed near livestock
•PARKING•	National Trust car park above Broad Haven Beach
•PUBLIC TOILETS•	At start and at Stackpole Quay

BACKGROUND TO THE WALK

The limestone headlands of St Govan's and Stackpole make up some of the most impressive coastline in South Pembrokeshire. Their grass-covered, plateau-like tops are very different to the relentlessly undulating ground covered by most of the coast path and, as a result, an excursion around this most southerly point of Pembrokeshire is uniquely relaxing. The cliffs, however, make up only a short section of a varied walk that crosses two of the region's finest beaches and also explores some beautiful inland waters. Broad Haven is often referred to as Broad Haven South, to avoid confusion with the town and beach of the same name in St Brides Bay.

Quiet Bay
The beach here is a broad gem of white sand, backed by rolling dunes and flanked by impressive headlands. Barafundle Bay is equally as picturesque, but also benefits from a lack of road access that keeps it relatively quiet for most of the year. The final attraction of this simple circuit is the three-fingered waterway that probes deeply inland from Broad Haven. The wooded shores and mirror-calm waters make a refreshing change from the wildness of the coast.

The Headlands
The cliffs between Linney Head, closed to the public as part of the MOD firing range, and Stackpole Head, which is visited on this walk, are made up of carboniferous limestone and comprise some of the best limestone coastal scenery in Britain. Exposed to the full force of the Atlantic at their feet, they are often overhanging and also contain many caves and blowholes. A few spectacular sea stacks have survived the battering and now stud the coast a short distance offshore – Church Rock, seen on this walk, just off Broad Haven Beach, is

one of the finest examples. The area is also one of the most popular rock climbing locations in the country.

Bosherston Lily Ponds

This series of interconnecting lakes was created at the turn of the 19th century by Baron Cawdor, once the owner of the Stackpole Estate. He dammed a small tidal creek which then flooded the three tributary valleys. Subsequent drifting of sand has created a large marram grass-covered dune system behind the beach. The lakes are abundant in wildlife, with herons prowling the shallows, swans, ducks, moorhens and coots all easily visible on the surface, and shyer creatures such as kingfishers often spotted. The Lily Ponds, which are made up of the two westerly fingers, are managed as a National Nature Reserve, and the lilies themselves are at their best in June, while the woodland is a magnificent spectacle in spring and autumn.

Walk 12 Directions

① From the car park, head back to the National Trust building at the head of the lane and bear right, down a set of steps, to the beach. Cross the beach and keep left to walk up the creek to a footbridge.

② Go over this and bear right to walk above rocky outcrops, above the beach, to a gate. Follow the grassy path around the headland and back inland to a stile above **Saddle Bay**. Continue around a large blowhole and up to a gate above a deeply cloven zawn (cleft), known as the **Raming Hole**.

③ Go through the gate and hug the coastline on your right to walk around **Stackpole Head**. As you turn back inland, pass a blowhole and then go through a gate to drop down to **Barafundle Bay**. Cross the back of the beach and climb up the steps on the other side to an archway in the wall. Continue around to **Stackpole Quay**.

④ Turn left, above the tiny harbour, to pass the **Old Boathouse**

WHERE TO EAT AND DRINK ⓘ

St Govan's Inn at Bosherston is a hidden gem, with great food and a selection of real ales. The walls are often decorated with photographs of climbers in seemingly impossible positions on the surrounding cliffs. Dogs allowed in bar.

Tearoom on your left before turning sharp right on to a road. Follow this past some buildings on the right and up to a T-junction, where you turn left.

⑤ Drop down into Stackpole village, pass the **Stackpole Inn** on the right, and continue around a series of bends until you come to a road on the left, over a bridge.

WHAT TO LOOK FOR ⓘ

The **views** east from Stackpole Head stretch from Caldey Island – a religious enclave just off the coast of Tenby – to the Gower Peninsula in the distance. Beyond, to the south, you may be able to make out the lofty landform of Lundy Island and even the outline of the North Devon coast.

---

⑥ Cross the bridge and bear left to follow a good path along the side of the lake. This leads through one kissing gate to a second, where you bear right, up a short steep section. At the top, bear left, on to a broad path with a wooden handrail. Follow this to a bridge.

⑦ Don't cross the bridge, but drop down on to a path and follow it with the lake on your left. Continue ahead to another bridge, cross it, then carry on with the lake now on your right. This path leads to the footbridge that you crossed at Point ②. Retrace your steps across the beach and up the steps back to the car park.

WHILE YOU'RE THERE ⓘ

Providing the footpath is open, take a stroll to **St Govan's Chapel**, a humble but spiritually uplifting stone building tucked away in a deep cleft in the cliffs, west of St Govan's Head. St Govan is thought to have been an Irish contemporary of St David and the story suggests that he was hiding from pirates in the cleft when a crack miraculously opened up in the floor. He entered and the crack then closed behind him, only opening again when the danger had passed. The present chapel dates from the 13th century, but probably incorporates some much older stonework.

Magnificent Manorbier and Swanlake Bay

A short stroll across open farmland then taking in some breathtaking coastal scenery.

•DISTANCE•	3 miles (4.8km)
•MINIMUM TIME•	1hr 30min
•ASCENT / GRADIENT•	290ft (88m) ▲▲▲
•LEVEL OF DIFFICULTY•	🚶 🚶 🚶
•PATHS•	Coast path, clear paths across farmland, 6 stiles
•LANDSCAPE•	Sandy coves and dramatic coastline
•SUGGESTED MAP•	aqua3 OS Explorer OL36 South Pembrokeshire
•START / FINISH•	Grid reference: SS 063976
•DOG FRIENDLINESS•	Difficult stiles, poop scoop on beaches. Keep on lead and off grass near house on The Dak
•PARKING•	Pay-and-display car park by beach below castle
•PUBLIC TOILETS•	At start

BACKGROUND TO THE WALK

This is a delightful short walk that runs along the heads of some magnificent cliffs and visits a wonderful and remote sandy cove. The outward leg isn't particularly inspirational, but the narrow lane provides convenient access to the highest ground and the section across farmland is open and breezy, with fine views over the coast. Once reached, the narrow belt of white sand that makes up Swanlake Bay provides ample reward for your efforts. Flanked on both sides by impressive sandstone crags and cut off from easy road access by the farmland that you've just traversed, it sees few visitors and provides a stunning setting for a picnic.

Gerald's Pleasant Spot

Once lauded by its most famous son, Giraldus Cambrensis, alias Gerald of Wales, as the 'pleasantest spot in Wales', Manorbier is these days best described as an attractive but sleepy coastal village dominated by a mighty castle and set among some of South Pembrokeshire's prettiest and most unspoilt countryside. Giraldus was born Gerald de Barri, the grandson of Odo, the first Norman Lord of the Manor, in 1146. He is best known for his attempts to set up an independent Church for Wales – a movement denied by Henry II – and for his chronicles of everyday life in both Wales and Ireland.

Caldey Island

The village name derives from 'Maenor of Pyrrus' or 'Manor of Pyr'. Pyrrus was the first Celtic abbot of Caldey, a nearby island first inhabited by monks in the 6th century AD and known in Welsh as Ynys Pyr, or Pyr's Island. Its landscape is wild and unspoilt and its buildings are inspirationally simple. There is a working Benedictine monastery and a number of ornate churches, including 12th-century St Illtud's, which houses a significant ancient sandstone cross.

Walk 13

Manorbier Castle

Despite the profusion of well-preserved castles in this corner of Pembrokeshire, it still comes as a surprise to discover such an impressive edifice tucked away in this tiny village. The original castle stems from the late 11th century, but the stone building that stands tall and proud over the beach and village these days was constructed in the early 12th century.

Many Owners

Since the De Barris, the castle has passed through many hands, including the Crown. It's now privately owned, but open to the public for tours. As well as the splendid views over the bay from the top of the castle walls, you'll also see many stately rooms, occupied these days by waxwork models of various figures, including Gerald, hard at work on his accounts.

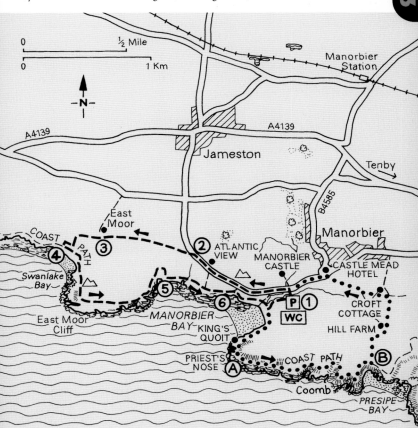

Walk 13 Directions

① Walk out of the car park entrance and then turn left on to the narrow lane. Follow this lane steeply upwards and bearing around to the right. You'll continue to climb above the coastline and pass the impressively situated and well-named **Atlantic View** cottage on your right before reaching a double gate and stile on your left.

Walk 13

② Cross the stile and walk along the field edge, with a bank and fence on your right, to reach a stone step stile. Cross the stile and continue heading in the same direction to a wooden stile which you also cross. Continue to a stone step stile by the farmhouse, which brings you into a small enclosure, then to a wooden stile that leads you away from the buildings.

③ Continue again along the edge of the field to another stone stile. Cross this stile and turn left to drop down the field edge to yet another stile that leads on to the **coast path**. Access to the beach is more or less directly beneath you.

④ Turn left on to the coast path and follow it over another stile and steeply uphill. You'll eventually reach the top on a lovely airy ridge

> **WHERE TO EAT AND DRINK** ⓘ
> The **Castle Inn**, in the centre of Manorbier, is a cosy and friendly place with a good selection of food and a decent choice of ales. It boasts a great garden where you can sit and relax after a hard morning or afternoon's walk.

> **WHAT TO LOOK FOR** ⓘ
> The cliffs along this part of the coast show some dramatic irregularities in the old red sandstone that forms them. **East Moor Cliff**, the eastern headland of Swanlake Bay, is a prime example, with huge blocks creating impressive bastions. There are a few low-grade rock climbs on the cliff, which is huge and split by a very deep fissure.

that swings east and then north to drop steeply down into a narrow dip above **Manorbier Bay**.

⑤ Cross another stile and climb out of the dip to continue walking easily above the rocky beach. This path leads to a drive, beneath a large house.

⑥ Continue beneath **The Dak** and uphill slightly, where the coast path drops off to the right. Follow this as it skirts a small car park and then winds down through the gorse and bracken to the beach. Cross the stream and turn left to follow a sandy track back to the car park.

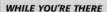

> **WHILE YOU'RE THERE** ⓘ
> **Tenby** is the unofficial tourism capital of South Pembrokeshire and although its crowded streets and rows of hotels and B&Bs come as something of a shock after the more organic spots along the coast, it's still a charming, mainly Georgian, town with a beautiful harbour and plenty of attractions to keep you busy on a rainy day. Of particular historical interest are the original town walls. They were so effective that the Norman castle was made pretty much redundant.

Walk 14

Coastline and Cove

An excellent extension that's a short walk in its own right.
See map and information panel for Walk 13

•DISTANCE•	5½ miles (8.8km)
•MINIMUM TIME•	2hrs 30min
•ASCENT / GRADIENT•	580ft (177m) ▲▲▲
•LEVEL OF DIFFICULTY•	🚶🚶 🚶 🚶

Walk 14 Directions (Walk 13 option)

Leave Walk 13 after crossing the stream beyond Point ⑥ and cross the back of the beach to a set of steps that lead up to the coast path. Climb up through the bracken on a narrow path that shortly passes the impressive **King's Quoit**, a Stone-Age burial chamber boasting a 16ft (4.8m) capstone supported by two smaller stones.

With fine views over Manorbier Beach and the sandstone headland crossed by Walk 13, continue up to the apex of the **Priest's Nose**, another sandstone headland with a number of caves (Point Ⓐ). The path now passes close to a series of deeply cloven zawns, then turns east again to carve a narrow walkway across the steep hillside. The cliffs are lined by many steep slabs and bulky blocks that take the full force of any swell running.

At **Coomb** the trail turns inland again to round a steep-sided valley. Climb away from this and continue back out on to the headland; again the cliffs are propped up by magnificent rock formations. Next comes **Presipe Bay**, a narrow strip of secluded, bleached sand that appears almost smothered beneath such impressive cliffs (Point Ⓑ). There's a wonderful viewpoint to the right of the path before it starts to descend. Access to the beach is via a set of steep steps in its western corner, but beware – the sands are pretty much covered at high tide so it's worth checking the timetable if you're hoping to spend time here.

Track back inland, above the bay, to a stile. Cross this and turn left, away from the coast, to walk up the edge of the field to another stile. Continue in the same direction to a small clump of trees where a waymarker points you diagonally right to another stile. Cross this and follow the grassy track around **Hill Farm** to a point where it swings left. Go over a stile on the right and walk directly across the field to a waymarker by a telegraph pole. Continue through a gap in the wall, across another field to another stile. Keep straight ahead to a gap in a large wall ahead and turn sharp left to cross a stile on to a surfaced drive. Pass **Croft Cottage** on your right and continue to a T-junction where you bear right. Follow this to the road, by the **Castle Mead Hotel**. Turn left to walk down the road, back to the car park at the start of Walk 13.

An Island Fling Around Dinas Head

A short, sharp and totally breathtaking circuit of a dramatic segregated headland.

Walk 15

•DISTANCE•	3 miles (4.8km)
•MINIMUM TIME•	2hrs
•ASCENT / GRADIENT•	460ft (140m) ▲▲ ▲ ▲
•LEVEL OF DIFFICULTY•	🚶🚶 🚶🚶 🚶🚶
•PATHS•	Rough coastal path and easy, wheelchair-friendly track, 4 stiles
•LANDSCAPE•	Rugged cliffs with views over two sweeping bays
•SUGGESTED MAP•	aqua3 OS Explorer OL35 North Pembrokeshire
•START / FINISH•	Grid reference: SN 004399
•DOG FRIENDLINESS•	Great dog walking area
•PARKING•	Both sides of road by Old Sailors, Pwllgwaelod Beach
•PUBLIC TOILETS•	At start and Cwm-yr-Eglwys

Walk 15 Directions

Dinas Island, or Dinas Head as it's often known (Dinas Head is actually the headland at the island's northern apex), isn't actually an island at all. It's a rugged, sloping peninsula that's separated from the mainland by a shallow neck of flat marshy ground known as Cwm Dewi. This was formed at the end of the last ice age when a glacier blocked the outlet of Newport Bay, forcing watercourses westwards, beneath the ice. The shales and

sandstone of the headland were eroded into a narrow channel. Island or not, this is a wonderful place to walk, encapsulating everything that's great about walking along a coast path for just an hour or so's effort.

From the car park, make your way to the beach and bear right to head towards the steep path on to **Dinas Island**. Pass the buildings on your right and turn right through a gate to gain a well-surfaced path that follows the floor of **Cwm Dewi**. This wheelchair-friendly track is very popular so you'll probably meet other walkers as you pass the marshy ground to the right.

These marshes are important breeding grounds for a number of butterflies. Common blues are small, with blue wings that have no black edges. Male orange-tips are a little like cabbage whites, but with orange tips to their wings. The

---

WHERE TO EAT AND DRINK ⓘ

The Old Sailor's licensed restaurant, adjacent to the car park, has replaced a pub called the Sailor's Safety Inn, which once showed a light to guide shipping. It specialises in seafood but it's also a good spot for a cream tea if that's all you need. Away from here, there's the popular **Ship Aground**, a grand public house in nearby Dinas Cross.

larger species of tortoiseshell and peacock are also regularly seen.

The path leads to a gate that in turn leads you through a caravan site and into the Cwm-yr-Eglwys car park. Turn left in the car park and follow a narrow path out towards the beach.

The ruins of the tiny **Chapel of St Bryanch** dominate a pleasant green above the beach. Sheltered from the prevailing south westerlies that pound this stretch of coast, Cwm-yr-Eglwys often has the feel of a quaint Mediterranean hamlet, but on the night of 25 October 1859, it was subjected to one of the fiercest storms on record. The church was almost completely destroyed – all that stands today are the west wall and the tiny belfry. However, this was only a small part of the damage wreaked. That same night, 114 ships were wrecked off the Welsh coast.

Keep the ruins to your right and wander along the lane to a coast path waymarker on the right. Follow this over a footbridge and then steeply up above **Aber Pig-y-Baw**. The path emerges from the bushes and continues to cut easily around the hillside before steepening as it approaches the obvious sea stack of **Needle Rock**. This is a fine nesting site for a variety of seabirds and it appears positively congested in late spring and early summer.

Steps lead up the hillside from here and then the path continues to climb until it reaches the **trig point** that marks the top of the headland. This is a wonderfully lofty viewpoint and it is possible to scramble down a little way to the north if you fancy a sheltered rest stop. The path now leads down above the western cliffs. Follow it to an obvious corner where a footpath forks off left through the inland fields. Ignore this and stay on the outside of the perimeter fence as it swings south again. Follow the coast down and wind your way through the gorse to a fork where the right-hand option heads out around **Pen Castell**. This tracks back inland again and drops to a stile above **Pwllgwaelod Beach**. From here you reach the road and can walk easily back past the **Old Sailor's** restaurant to the beach and the car park.

WHILE YOU'RE THERE   ⓘ

If the spiritual side of West Wales grabs your attention, you may enjoy the **Saints and Stones Trail**, a waymarked, driving tour of some of the finest churches and religious sites in the area, many dating back to pre-Christian times. As well as St David's Cathedral, other highlights include the bleeding yew in St Brynach's (► Walk 16). Leaflets describing the trail, which makes a big loop between Fishguard and St David's, are available from all the local tourist offices.

WHAT TO LOOK FOR   ⓘ

The black and white birds usually seen on the steeper inner cliff of Needle Rock are **guillemots** and **razorbills**. Both are members of the auk family and it is difficult to tell them apart from a distance. The guillemot is actually a beautiful dark-chocolate colour and has a slim pointed bill, while the razorbill is more black in colour and close inspection of the head reveals that the bill is razor shaped, with thin white lines. You'll probably also notice a number of **herring gulls** on the fringes of the mêlée. These raucous gulls scavenge relentlessly, feeding on the eggs and chicks of the smaller auks. They will even steal the food from the parent birds' mouths.

Walk with Angels Above Newport

A coastal exploration of Pembrokeshire's Newport and a stiff climb on to one of Britain's most sacred hilltops.

•DISTANCE•	5½ miles (8.8km)
•MINIMUM TIME•	3hrs 30min
•ASCENT / GRADIENT•	1,080ft (329m) ▲▲▲
•LEVEL OF DIFFICULTY•	🚶🚶 🚶🚶 🚶
•PATHS•	Easy coastal footpaths, boggy farm tracks, rough paths over bracken and heather-covered hillsides, 2 stiles
•LANDSCAPE•	Attractive harbour, farmland and rock-capped moor
•SUGGESTED MAP•	aqua3 OS Explorer OL35 North Pembrokeshire
•START / FINISH•	Grid reference: SN 057392
•DOG FRIENDLINESS•	Care on roads, poop scoop on coast path section
•PARKING•	Free car park opposite information centre, Long Street
•PUBLIC TOILETS•	At start and near Parrog

BACKGROUND TO THE WALK

Carn Ingli appears to peep over the shoulder of the small coastal town of Newport in the same way as Table Mountain does in Cape Town, South Africa. The domination of the town's skyline by the bold, rock-capped summit seems to make them inseparable and it therefore makes sense to explore both in one walk. The coastal section is easy to follow and thoroughly enjoyable as the path traces a varied line along the Nyfer Estuary, at one stage following the actual sea wall itself. The tracks that cross the common, on the other hand, are rough and, in late summer, when the bracken is fully-grown, difficult to follow in places. They're worth sticking with though, for the views from the jagged rocks of the peak are among the best in the Pembrokeshire Coast National Park.

Newport

Once a busy port immersed predominantly in the wool trade, Newport was the former capital of the Marcher Lordship of Cemmaes, the only one to escape the abolition imposed by Henry VIII in the 16th-century Acts of Union. William Fitz-martin, who moved to Newport from nearby Nevern, granted a number of privileges to the town, including the election of its own mayor, something which it still has to this day, and the beating of the bounds on horseback by the mayor, which takes place every August. Its castle, once the home of the aforementioned lord, has since been incorporated into a mansion house and is now in private ownership.

The Rock of Angels

Often described as one of the most sacred sites in Britain, the lofty heights of Carn Ingli were well known by the mystical St Brynach, who scaled them in order to commune with angels. After a life of persecution – the Irish-born saint was made most unwelcome by the Welsh when he returned from his pilgrimage to the Holy Land – he finally settled in Nevern, where he built his church. It remains one of the most visited in Pembrokeshire due to its ancient Celtic cross and a yew tree that appears to actually bleed. A second cross, carved into the rocky hillside, has seen so many visitors that the stones beneath it are now as smooth as glass. Scientific evidence has supported the theories of the hill's special powers; rainbows have been witnessed at night and wild magnetic deviations on the summit have been known to point a compass needle due south.

Judging from the remains of both Iron-Age fortresses and Bronze-Age huts, there was human activity on Mynydd Carningli long before Christianity. The size of the settlements suggests that the windswept hillside would have once supported fairly large communities. Perhaps the existence of standing stones near by demonstrates that these settlers were also aware of the mountain's special powers.

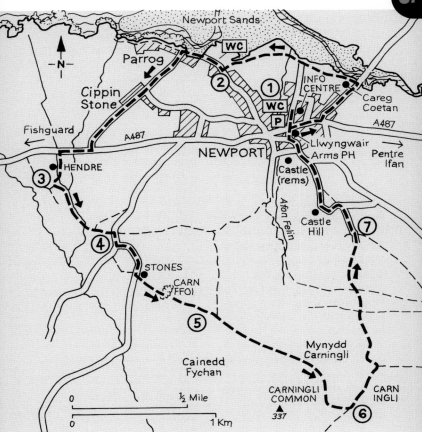

Walk 16 **Directions**

① Turn right out of the car park and left on to the **High Street**. Fork left into **Pen y Bont** and continue to the bridge, where a waymarked

footpath leads off to the left. Follow this along the banks of the estuary to a small road.

② Turn right on the road and walk past the toilets to its end, where the path then follows the sea wall.

Continue to another lane and turn left to follow it to the **A487**. Turn right on to this road, then turn left to continue walking up the drive of **Hendre farm**.

③ Go through the gate, to the left of the buildings, and follow the track across a small stream. The path hugs the left edge of the field to reach another gate. Continue in the same line along a hedged section, which is boggy for most of the year. Keep straight ahead at the stile to climb up to the road.

WHERE TO EAT AND DRINK ⓘ

The **Llwyngwair Arms** is one of the best pubs in this part of Pembrokeshire, with good beer and a local but friendly atmosphere. In the evening it offers a wonderful range of very authentic tasting Indian dishes, in addition to the usual pub grub.

---

④ Turn right on to the road and then fork left to continue past some houses to a pair of huge stones on the left. Pass through these stones and follow the faint track up to a rocky tor. Head up from this towards the larger tor of **Carn Ffoi**. From here you'll be able to pick up a clearer path that leads on to a broken wall.

⑤ Pass through the remains of the wall and follow the clear footpath across the hillside, aiming towards the obvious top of **Carn Ingli**, which rises ahead of you. Pass

beneath the highpoint of **Carningli Common**, where you'll see a faint footpath on the right-hand side heading up towards a shallow saddle. Take this footpath and then, as the ground levels off, bear left to follow any of the faint tracks that lead up on to the ridge.

⑥ Follow the ridge line northwards and drop down, again on faint footpaths, to join a good, clear track that runs straight down the hillside. Continue on this, keeping straight ahead at two crossroads, then turn left and then right when you get to the next junction. This drops you down to a gate in a corner, which leads on to a lane.

⑦ Take the lane to a crossroads and keep straight ahead to walk past a house to an obvious sunken track. Follow this down to a drive and turn left, then right, on to **Church Street**. Continue into the centre and go straight across the main road into **Long Street**.

WHAT TO LOOK FOR ⓘ

On your left, as you approach the bridge along Pen-y-Bont, you'll find the rather understated **Careg Coetan**, an impressive cromlech or burial chamber tucked away behind holiday bungalows. In common with many such sites in Wales, it's said to be the final resting place of the legendary King Arthur. The site may be as much as 5,000 years old and excavation by archaeologists revealed cremation remains beneath it.

WHILE YOU'RE THERE ⓘ

Small lanes lead east from Newport to Pentre Ifan, one of the finest **megalithic cromlechs** in the British Isles. Over 4,000 years old, the giant 16ft (4.8m) capstone sits on a selection of smaller supports that hold it some 6ft (1.8m) above ground. It is thought that the builders of these magnificent tombs believed by constructing them on high ground the interred souls of the dead would be placed closer to the spirits and the bringer of life, the sun. It would have originally been covered with a mound of earth, but this has since eroded away.

Romancing the Stones in the Preseli Hills

Easy walking to a spectacular hill around some of the most mystical rocks on the planet.

•DISTANCE•	5½ miles (8.8km)
•MINIMUM TIME•	2hrs 30min
•ASCENT / GRADIENT•	560ft (170m) ▲▲▲
•LEVEL OF DIFFICULTY•	🚶🚶 🚶🚶 🚶🚶
•PATHS•	Mainly clear paths across open moorland, no stiles
•LANDSCAPE•	Rolling hills topped with rocky outcrops
•SUGGESTED MAP•	aqua3 OS Explorer OL35 North Pembrokeshire
•START / FINISH•	Grid reference: SO 165331
•DOG FRIENDLINESS•	Care needed near livestock
•PARKING•	Small lay-by on lane beneath Foeldrygarn
•PUBLIC TOILETS•	None on route but plenty of sheltered nooks and crannies
•NOTE•	Navigation very difficult in poor visibility

· BACKGROUND TO THE WALK

A circular walk around the most interesting sites of the Preseli Hills is almost impossible. The uplands form an isolated east–west ridge that would at best form one side of a circuit linked with a lengthy road section. Instead of taking this less-than-ideal option, this walk forms a contorted and narrow figure-of-eight that scales the most spectacular hill on the ridge, traces the line of the famous dolerite outcrops, or carns, and then makes an out-and-back sortie to an impressive stone circle. Convoluted it may be, but it's packed with interest and easy going enough for most people to complete comfortably.

Preseli Hills

The Pembrokeshire Coast National Park is best known for its stunning coastline. Britain's smallest National Park is in no single place further than 10 miles (16.1km) from the sea. This furthest point was a deliberate extension of the boundaries to incorporate one of the most important historic sites in the United Kingdom, the Preseli Hills.

Carn Menyn's Bluestones

It was from Carn Menyn, one of the rocky tors that crown the marshy and often windswept hills, that the bluestones forming the inner circle of Stonehenge were taken. These bluestones, or spotted dolerite stones to give them their proper name, would have each weighed somewhere in the region of 4 tonnes and must have been transported over 200 miles (320km) in total. To this day we cannot explain how or why.

Ancient Road

The Stonehenge story, significant as it may be, is only part of the historic and, at times, mystical feel of this narrow, grassy upland. The track that follows the ridge is an ancient road, perhaps dating back over 5,000 years. It's probable that it was a safe passage between the coast and the settlements inland at a time when wild predators such as bears and wolves roamed the valleys below. Gravestones line the track, most likely those of travellers or traders who were buried where they died, and other standing stones dot the hillsides.

Beddarthur

West of Carn Menyn, beneath another impressive outcrop named Carn Bica, there's a stone circle known as Beddarthur. Small by comparison to Stonehenge or Avebury, its oval arrangement of 2ft–3ft (0.6m–1m) high stones is said to be yet another burial place of King Arthur; 'bedd' means grave in Welsh. There are certainly links between the legendary historical superhero and the area; it's suggested that the King and his knights chased Twrch Trywyth, the magical giant boar, across these hills before heading east.

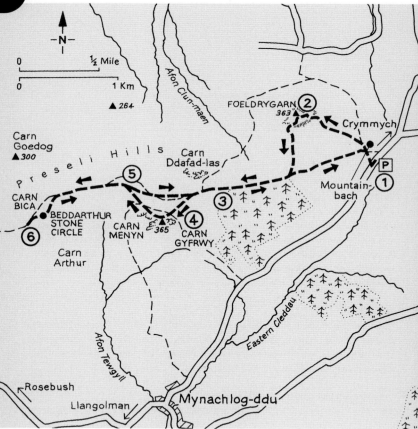

Walk 17 Directions

① Walk to the right out of the lay-by on the lane from **Crymych**, then turn right up a stony track. When you reach the gate, keep going straight ahead for another 100yds (91m) or so, and then fork left on to a grassy track, which soon becomes clearer as it winds its way up the hillside. Follow this all the way to the rocky cairns and trig point on **Foeldrygarn**.

WHILE YOU'RE THERE ℹ️

Slate quarrying was once big business in the Preseli Hills and the remnants of this activity are still visible in places like Rosebush, to the west. If you'd like to see the kind of thing that can be crafted out of the smooth, flat stones, take a look at the **Slate Workshop** at Llangolman, where authentic Welsh slate is still put to good effect in a variety of craft items.

② Bear left at the summit and locate a grassy track that drops to the south. Cross the heather-clad plateau beneath, aiming for the left-hand corner of a wood. When you meet the main track, turn right to walk with the edge of the wood on your left.

③ Leaving the wood, the path climbs slightly to some rocky tors. The second of these, the one that's closest to the track, has a sheepfold at its base. Shortly after this, the path forks and you follow the left-hand track down to the nearest of the group of outcrops to your left.

④ This is **Carn Gyfrwy**. Continue on faint paths to the larger outcrops ahead, then curve right and drop slightly to **Carn Menyn**, the lowest of the bunch, perched precariously on the edge of the escarpment. The path becomes clearer here and

drops slightly into a marshy saddle that can be seen ahead.

⑤ In the saddle you'll meet the main track. Turn left and follow it steadily up towards **Carn Bica**, which is visible on the hillside ahead of you. Just before this, you'll cross the circle made by the stones of **Beddarthur**.

⑥ Turn around and retrace your steps back to the saddle. Climb slightly to pass the tor with the sheepfold and stay on this main path to walk beside the plantation once more, now on your right. At the end of this, drop, on a grassy track, down to the gate. Turn right on to the lane and continue back to the car park.

WHERE TO EAT AND DRINK ℹ️

There's nothing on the route so it's best to head west to Rosebush where the **Tafarn Sinc** does good food and welcomes children in the eating area before 9PM. There's also decent food to be found at the **New Inn** (Tafarn Newydd) on the main road on the other side of the village.

WHAT TO LOOK FOR ℹ️

Foeldrygarn translates to 'the rounded or bare hill of three cairns', and when you reach the summit you'll easily see why. As well as the concrete trig point, the rounded summit is adorned with three huge piles of stones that were at one time giant Bronze-Age **burial cairns**. The summit is also guarded by the visible remains of the ramparts of an Iron-Age fort.

The Highs and Lows of Rhossili Bay

This walk takes in the stunning views over one of Wales's finest and wildest beaches.

•DISTANCE•	4 miles (6.4km)
•MINIMUM TIME•	1hr 45min
•ASCENT / GRADIENT•	590ft (180m) ▲▲ ▲▲ ▲
•LEVEL OF DIFFICULTY•	🚶🚶 🚶🚶 🚶🚶
•PATHS•	Easy-to-follow footpaths across grassy downs, 2 stiles
•LANDSCAPE•	Rolling downland, rocky outcrops and views over gorgeous sandy beach
•SUGGESTED MAP•	aqua3 OS Explorer 164 Gower
•START / FINISH•	Grid reference: SS 416880
•DOG FRIENDLINESS•	Care needed near livestock
•PARKING•	Large car park at end of road in Rhossili
•PUBLIC TOILETS•	At start

BACKGROUND TO THE WALK

Of all the Gower walks this is my favourite, although rather oddly, in its short form, your feet won't leave a single footprint in the sand. The lofty heights of Rhossili Down not only show the magnificent arc of sand in its best light, but they also offer a feeling of spaciousness that's difficult to describe and almost impossible to equal in this part of the world. The ancient stones that define the ridge line only add to the captivating atmosphere.

Area of Outstanding Natural Beauty

The Gower Peninsula comprises a 15-mile (24km) finger of land that points westwards from the urban sprawl of Swansea. Its southern coast is the more spectacular, boasting dune-backed beaches of surf-swept, clean, yellow sand and magnificent limestone cliffs, chiselled in places into deep gullies and knife-edge ridges. The northern coast forms the southern fringes of the marshy Loughor Estuary. It's nothing like as dramatic as the southern coast, but it's an important habitat for wading birds and other marine life. Between the two coastlines, the land rises into a series of whaleback ridges, or downs, covered with gorse, heather and bracken and littered with prehistoric stones and remains. Scattered around the windswept landscape are a number of impressive castles. In 1957, the peninsula was designated Britain's first Area of Outstanding Natural Beauty (AONB).

Rhossili Bay and Down

Of all the Gower beaches, none are blessed with quite the untamed splendour of Rhossili Bay. It's sweeping expanse of golden sand runs for over 4 miles (6.4km) from the headland of the Worms Head to the stranded outcrop of Burry Holms, upon which sits a ruined monastic chapel. It owes much of its wild nature to the steep-sided down that presides over its relentless waves and provides a natural and impenetrable barrier to development. The down is a 633ft (193m) high, whaleback ridge that runs almost the full length of the beach.

The path that traces the ridge is one the fairest places to walk in the whole of South Wales, especially in late summer when the heather tinges the hillsides pink. From The Beacon, at the southern end of the ridge, the views stretch far beyond the coastline at your feet and it's often possible to see St Govan's Head in Pembrokeshire and even the North Devon coastline on a very clear day.

The Worms Head

The string of tiny islets that thrust defiantly into the Atlantic at the bay's southernmost tip are known as the Worms Head. This doesn't refer to the earthworm, but is a derivative of the Old English, Orm, which means dragon or serpent. The likeness can be seen. It is now a nature reserve, but can be reached at low tide by scrambling across the rocky causeway at the western tip of the promontory. It's essential that you check the tide timetables before making such a sortie as it's easy to be cut off by the surprising tenacity of the rising tides.

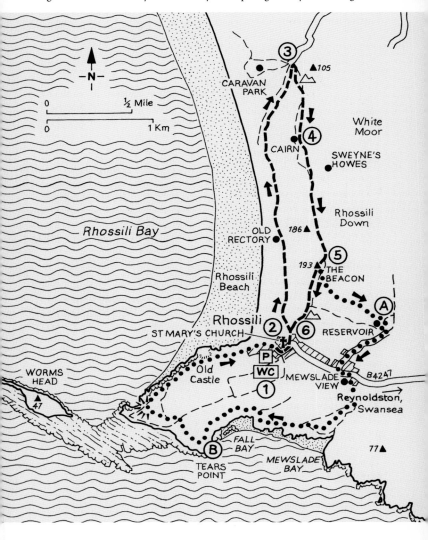

Walk 18 Directions

① From the car park, head out on to the road and continue uphill as if you were walking back out of the village. You'll pass **St Mary's Church** on your left then, immediately after this, bear left down on a broad track to a gate. Go through the gate and keep left to follow a grassy track that snakes along the steep hillside.

WHILE YOU'RE THERE ⓘ
About ½ mile (800m) east of Reynoldston there's a footpath that leads to **King Arthur's Stone**, one of the finest standing cromlechs (burial chambers) in Wales, covered with an enormous capstone. The site is believed to be over 6,000 years old and is most striking when visited at sunrise or sunset.

② Follow this through the bracken, passing the **Old Rectory** on your left and eventually you'll reach a sunken section with a wall on your left, and a **caravan park** behind. Don't be tempted to break off right just yet; instead, keep going until you come to a gate.

③ Turn sharp right here and follow the grassy track steeply up on to the ridge. At the top of the steep section it's easy to be drawn off to the right towards some obvious outcrops, but keep to the top track that literally follows the crest.

④ You'll pass some ancient cairns and drop slightly to pass a pair of megalithic cromlechs, or burial chambers. These are known as **Sweyne's Howes** and are over 4,000 years old. Continue on a broad track up to the high point of **The Beacon**.

⑤ Keep straight ahead on a clear track that starts to drop easily then steepens to meet a dry-stone wall. Continue walking down the side of the wall and you'll eventually come to the gate you passed through on the way out.

WHAT TO LOOK FOR ⓘ
More than one ship has fallen foul of the cruel storms that pound Rhossili and the **wreckage** of a few of these still pepper the beach. The most obvious is the *Helvetica*, now a crumbled timber skeleton protruding from the sands at low tide. She was washed up here in November 1887, but miraculously her five-man crew all survived.

⑥ Follow the lane out to the road, turn right and pass **St Mary's Church** on your right to return to the car park.

WHERE TO EAT AND DRINK ⓘ
There are a few places to get a cuppa and a snack in Rhossili; from the **Bay View Shop**, which offers hot snacks and has a few tables outside to the **Rendezvous Café**, which acts as a tea room during the day and a full-blown restaurant at night. The **Worms Head Hotel** is the only pub in the village, but if you don't mind driving a few miles, the **King Arthur Hotel** at Reynoldston has a better atmosphere and serves better food.

Rhossili and Mewslade Bay

Extend the walk to dip your toes in the water in Mewslade Bay.
See map and information panel for Walk 18

•DISTANCE•	7 miles (11.3km)
•MINIMUM TIME•	3hrs
•ASCENT / GRADIENT•	650ft (198m) ▲▲▲
•LEVEL OF DIFFICULTY•	🚶🚶🚶

Walk 19 Directions (Walk 18 option)

While Walk 18 reveals the magnificent sweep of Rhossili Bay, what it doesn't show are the rugged limestone bluffs and headlands that make up the bulk of the peninsula's southern coast. For that reason, providing you've got both the energy and the time, it's well worth descending to the left of the trig point and dropping down to the rocky gash that forms the secluded Mewslade Bay (a trip to the beach is optional). Returning to Rhossili from here, you get a taster of the rugged rock-strewn landscape that's explored in more detail in Walk 20 and you also get a bird's-eye view over the Gower's most distinctive landmark, the rocky islets of the Worms Head.

From the trig point on **The Beacon** (Point ⑤), bear around to the left and follow the track easily down a blunt spur of the hill. You'll see a covered reservoir on your right where you'll pick up the head of a gravel track. Follow this beneath the **reservoir** (Point Ⓐ) and down to a lane, where you turn right. Follow the lane down to the **B4247** and cross the road. Turn left on to the pavement and follow this along until, after a cottage called **Mewslade View**, you turn right on to a hedged lane. Follow this down to a gate. Continue straight ahead if you fancy getting your toes wet; if not, turn right on to the bracken-covered heathland.

The path drops into a shallow dip and then forks. Take the left-hand track, which heads uphill through the bracken on to an open headland above **Mewslade Bay**. Follow the coast around to the right and pass through some spectacular limestone outcrops and above some impressive cliffs before being funnelled into a narrow section by a wall. The path is obvious from this point as it crosses above **Fall Bay** and then climbs up towards **Tears Point**, Point Ⓑ. Continue to hug the wall until it dips into a valley, then bear slightly left to follow the cliffs around to the western end of the headland.

If the tides are right, it's possible to drop down from here to cross on to the **Worms Head**. If not, bear right and follow the path along the cliff line until it meets the wall again. From here, continue easily back towards **Rhossili** on a well-surfaced track that leads to the road and on to the car park at Point ①.

Walk 20

From Port Eynon to Rhossili

A linear trek along a scenic stretch of the Gower coast returning by bus.

•DISTANCE•	6½ miles (10.4km)
•MINIMUM TIME•	3hrs
•ASCENT / GRADIENT•	850ft (260m) ▲▲▲
•LEVEL OF DIFFICULTY•	👫 👫 👫
•PATHS•	Coast path, 8 stiles
•LANDSCAPE•	Limestone cliffs and sheltered bays
•SUGGESTED MAP•	aqua3 OS Explorer 164 Gower
•START•	Grid reference: SS 467851
•FINISH•	Grid reference: SS 416881
•DOG FRIENDLINESS•	Generally fine on bus, care around livestock
•PARKING•	Large car park in Port Eynon
•PUBLIC TOILETS•	At start and at Rhossili

Walk 20 Directions

Walk past the pay-and-display machine and follow a broad sandy track through a gate and along to a kissing gate. Go through this, across the track that leads to the youth hostel and through another kissing gate towards the ruins of the **Salt House**, where an information board gives plenty of interesting history on the area. Follow the sandy track along the coast until, in the centre of the rocky bay to your left, the path splits. Take the right-hand fork and climb up steeply past a quarry on your right to the monument on the hilltop.

Follow the cliff tops until the path drops down to a stile. Cross this and walk behind the rocky beach. When the path forks, keep right to climb slightly, then drop left, down some steps to a second stile. Cross this and follow the path as it squeezes between impressive limestone cliffs and steep scree. You'll hurdle a wonderful rocky

terrace and drop beneath more formidable crags, many of which make for excellent rock climbing. The path sneaks between more rocky outcrops before heading down to a broken wall. Cross the wall and turn right to climb steeply upwards, then bear left around more outcrops to follow the apex of the valley up to meet a good path.

> ### WHERE TO EAT AND DRINK ⓘ
> Port Eynon is probably worse off than Rhossili for refreshments with the only pub, the **Ship**, being very touristy and not particularly good. There are a few snack options around the beach – the **Seafarer** chippie will do if you're after really casual or the **Smuggler's Haunt** tea rooms if you want something a little more civilised. Alternatively eat in Rhossili or travel to Reynoldston (► Where To Eat And Drink, Walk 18).

Turn left on to this and follow the wall. This section will fly by as you are saved any real drops or climbs until you reach the deeply cloven gorge of **Foxhole Slade**. Cross the iron stile in the dip and climb steeply back up. This area is owned by the National Trust and to your right, but almost impossible to reach, is **Paviland Cave**, where a headless body was once discovered. It was originally thought to be female and nicknamed the Red Lady of Paviland, as the bones were stained red. Subsequent modern-day tests show that the skeleton was actually male and carbon dating puts it at some 24,000 years old. Exploration of the area above the cave, which isn't safe to reach, reveals the ditches and ramparts of an ancient settlement. Continue along the wall and cross a fairly rickety stile. After 200yds (183m), next to a wooden gate on the right, fork left. Don't be drawn out on to the coast; instead continue in the same direction as the path starts until you join the wall again and drop to a stile.

Cross this and bear left to head back out on to the cliff top, where you'll find the obvious earthworks of an Iron-Age fort. A wall unceremoniously splits the ramparts; cross this by a stile and follow the coast around to a fence, which you then follow to the head of a huge hollow with no name on the OS map. Go behind this and continue along the line of the wall, which initially hugs the coast before heading back inland a little as it approaches **Mew Slade**. There are more ancient earthworks on **Thurba Head**, to your left. As the wall turns sharp right, keep straight ahead to a steep path that drops down awkwardly into Mew Slade.

At the bottom of the dip, turn left and follow a grassy path coastwards to a stile on the right. Cross this to gain access to the small cove, hidden behind rocky outcrops and

covered almost completely by the sea at high tide. A narrow path heads west from the beach and contours around the steep hillside to rejoin the main coast path in an area of outstanding limestone scenery. Bear left on to the path here and follow it around to another dip, where a path to the left has been closed due to cliff erosion. Keep high to round the head of the valley and then drop down, with the wall on your right, towards **Tears Point**. Here, leave the wall and head back up the grassy down towards the cliff tops, where you veer around to the right to follow them along. The main path actually hugs the wall all the way back to **Rhossili**, but a more enjoyable option is to continue around the coast passing above the **Worms Head** and then swinging north at **Kitchen Corner** to rejoin the main, well-surfaced track as you approach Rhossili village. Continue past the information centre and the main car park to the bus stop, on the left just before the church. There are five buses a day in each direction weekdays and a circular shuttle service at weekends (in season).

Woodland and Family Wars at Oxwich Point

A short but very exhilarating ramble through woodland and along delightful coastline.

•DISTANCE•	4½ miles (7.2km)
•MINIMUM TIME•	2hrs
•ASCENT / GRADIENT•	480ft (146m) ▲▲▲
•LEVEL OF DIFFICULTY•	𝕩𝕩 𝕩𝕩 𝕩𝕩
•PATHS•	Clear paths through woodland, along coast and across farmland, quiet lane, 6 stiles
•LANDSCAPE•	Mixed woodland and rugged coastline
•SUGGESTED MAP•	aqua3 OS Explorer 164 Gower
•START / FINISH•	Grid reference: SS 500864
•DOG FRIENDLINESS•	Can mostly run free
•PARKING•	Oxwich Bay
•PUBLIC TOILETS•	At car park near start

BACKGROUND TO THE WALK

The Gower has less obvious headlands than nearby Pembrokeshire and this makes it much more difficult to fashion short but interesting circular walks. This one stands out for a couple of reasons. Firstly, it can be combined with a visit to Oxwich National Nature Reserve, a treasure trove of marshland and sand dunes in a wonderful beachside location. Secondly, the wonderful coastal scenery includes the beautiful and usually deserted beach known as The Sands. And finally, being short, it allows plenty of time for exploring both the atmospheric St Illtud's Church and the majestic ruins of Oxwich Castle.

Oxwich Village

Once a busy port that paid its way by shipping limestone from quarries on the rugged headland, Oxwich is now one of the prettiest and most unspoilt Gower villages, due in no small part to its distance from the main roads. The name is derived from Axwick, Norse for Water Creek. For maximum enjoyment, it's best visited away from the main holiday seasons.

St Illtud's

Founded in the 6th century AD and tucked away in a leafy clearing above the beach, St Illtud's Church is particularly significant for its stone font, which is said to have been donated by St Illtud himself. The grounds are tranquil with an atmosphere that comes in stark contrast to the summertime chaos of the beach below. Behind the building is the grave of an unknown soldier who was washed up on the beach during World War Two. It's certainly a spooky spot and the graveyard is purported to be haunted by a strange half-man-half-horse creature.

St Illtud (or St Illtyd) was a Welsh-born monk who founded the nearby abbey of Llan-Illtut (Llantwit Major). He is perhaps most famous for his fights against famine which included sailing grain ships to Brittany. He died in Brittany in AD 505.

Feuding Families

Really a 16th-century mansion house built by Sir Rhys Mansel on the site of the 14th-century castle, Oxwich Castle occupies an airy setting above the bay. Sir Rhys, in common with many Gower locals, wasn't above plundering the cargo of ships that came to grief in the bay and was quick to take advantage of a French wreck in late December 1557. The salvage rights, however, belonged to a Sir George Herbert of Swansea, who quickly paid Mansel a visit to reclaim his goods. A fight broke out and Sir Rhys's daughter Anne was injured by a stone thrown by Herbert's servant. She later died from her injuries. Court action against Herbert proved ineffective and there followed a feud which continued for many years until eventually the Mansel family moved to Margam, east of Swansea. Part of the mansion was leased to local farmers, but most of the fine building fell into disrepair.

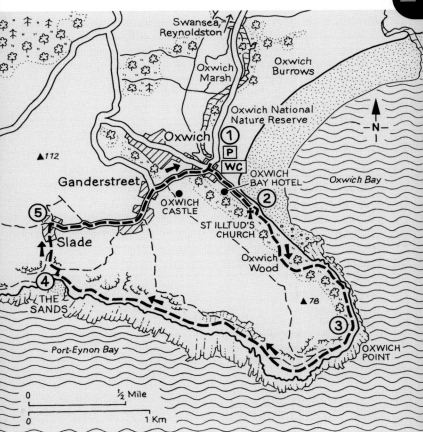

Walk 21 Directions

① Walk back out of the car park and turn left to a crossroads. Turn left here (waymarked 'Eglwys') and pass the **Woodside Guesthouse** and the **Oxwich Bay Hotel**, on your right. This lane leads into the woods and up to 6th-century **St Illtud's Church**, where a gate marks the end of the road and the start of a path leading out on to Oxwich Point.

Walk 21

② Go through the gate and bear right, going up the wooden steps to climb steeply up through the wood. As the footpath levels, bear left to drop back down through the wood and around the headland until it comes out into the open above **Oxwich Point**.

③ The path drops through gorse and bracken to become a grassy coast path that runs easily above a rocky beach. Keep the sea on your left and ignore any tracks that run off to the right. After approximately 1 mile (1.6km) you'll pass a distinct valley that drops in from your right. Continue past this and cross a succession of stiles, until you reach the sandy beach of **The Sands**.

④ Turn right, behind the beach, and follow a narrow footpath to a stile. This leads on to a broad farm track, where you turn left. Continue up and around to the right until you come to a galvanised kissing gate. Go through this and keep right to head up a lane past some houses to a crossroads.

> **WHERE TO EAT AND DRINK** ⓘ
> Snacks are available in Oxwich – try the **Beach Hut** or the **General Stores** – and there's also the **Oxwich Bay Hotel**, which you pass on the walk, serving food all day from bar snacks to daily specials (children's meals also available). But, for the best food and atmosphere in this part of the Gower, it's worth heading to the **King Arthur Hotel** in Reynoldston.

⑤ Turn right here and follow the road along to a fork where you keep right. Drop down to the entrance of **Oxwich Castle** on the right. After looking at or exploring the castle, turn right, back on to the lane, and head down into **Oxwich** village. Keep straight ahead to the car park.

> **WHAT TO LOOK FOR** ⓘ
> Spring is a great time to wander the woods of Oxwich Point where many interesting flowers can be seen vying for space before the deciduous canopy develops, cutting out the light supply. Perhaps the most prolific is **ramsons**, or wild garlic as it's also known. It isn't actually related to garlic, but when the woodland floor is completely carpeted by the stunning white flowers, the smell certainly resembles it.

> **WHILE YOU'RE THERE** ⓘ
> A windswept pot-pourri of dunes, saltwater marshes and freshwater pools, **Oxwich National Nature Reserve** offers an unusual and important habitat to many species of flora and fauna. Wild orchids are prolific in spring and early summer and the reserve is also an important breeding ground for a few species of butterfly, including the small blue, brown argus and marbled white. There are a number of trails that cross the marshes.

An Easy Stroll Along the Heritage Coast

A pleasant foray through rolling sand dunes, returning along the impressive and little-known South Wales coast.

•DISTANCE•	6 miles (9.7km)
•MINIMUM TIME•	2hrs 30min
•ASCENT / GRADIENT•	460ft (140m) ▲▲ ▲ ▲
•LEVEL OF DIFFICULTY•	🚶🚶 🚶🚶 🚶🚶
•PATHS•	Easy-to-follow across farmland and coastline, 5 stiles
•LANDSCAPE•	Deciduous woodland, farmland, bracken-covered sand dunes and rocky coastline
•SUGGESTED MAP•	aqua3 OS Explorer 151 Cardiff & Bridgend
•START / FINISH•	Grid reference: SS 885731
•DOG FRIENDLINESS•	Some difficult stiles; total ban on beach at Dunraven in summer
•PARKING•	Large car park at Heritage Centre above Dunraven Beach
•PUBLIC TOILETS•	Heritage Centre, also at Ogmore

BACKGROUND TO THE WALK

Most visitors to South Wales overlook the chunk of land that lies south of the M4 motorway between Cardiff and Swansea. Yet surprisingly, smack bang between the two cities and overshadowed by the huge industrial complexes of Port Talbot, there lies a sumptuous strip of coast that remains refreshingly unspoilt.

Glamorgan Heritage Coast
Granted Heritage Coast status in 1972, the 14-mile (22.5km) stretch of coastline that runs between Ogmore and Gileston stands as defiant against progress as its cliffs do against the huge ebbs and flows of the Bristol Channel tides. Sandy beaches, often punctuated by weathered strips of rock that dip their toes in the ocean, break up an otherwise formidable barrier of limestone and shale cliffs that rise and dip gracefully above the turbulent grey waters. It's fair to say that the scenery doesn't quite match the breathtaking beauty of the Gower Peninsula or Pembrokeshire, but somehow the unkempt wildness has an appeal all of it's own.

Heritage Centre
Dunraven Bay houses the Heritage Centre, which offers displays and information about the area. It also makes an appropriate starting point for a walk that gives at least a taster of this unique landscape. The early stages track inland, through woodland and farmland before heading coastwards, at the small village of St Brides Major. From here, the path sneaks between dunes and drops to the Ogmore River. Following the estuary downstream through bracken that simply teems with wildlife, you'll meet the coast at Ogmore-by-Sea and pick up the coast path above one of many beaches here. With ocean views to your right and the dunes to your left, you'll now climb easily back up above Dunraven where, if you time it

right, you'll witness the cliffs reflecting the pastel shades of sunset as you enjoy the final drop to the beach. It's a wonderful way to finish off an evening stroll.

Pilot Scheme
The Glamorgan Heritage Coast was one of three pilot schemes set up in 1972 to protect the country's unique coastal landscapes and environments from destructive development. There are now 43 such areas in England and Wales, and in Wales they account for over 40 per cent of the total coastline. The aims of the scheme are fourfold; to maintain the ecological diversity, to provide public access and encourage recreational use, to protect the needs of the local population, including farmers and landowners, and to preserve the quality of the coastline. The Glamorgan Heritage Coast is managed by the Countryside Council for Wales which employs a professional ranger service to take care of the day-to-day running of the area.

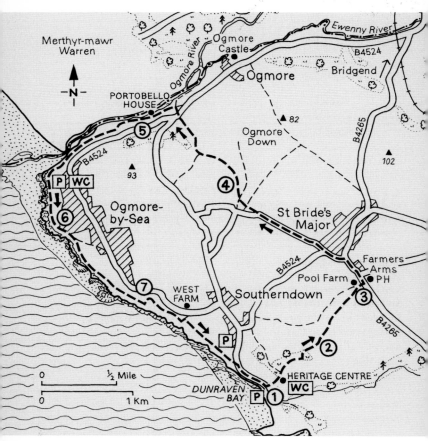

Walk 22 Directions

① Head up the lane at the back of the car park and pass the **Heritage Centre** on your right. Keep straight ahead on a narrow path that ducks into woodland and continue on this path to a stile. Cross the stile and walk along the edge of the field to reach a gate on your left. Go through the gate, then cross a stile on your right to continue with the hedge to your right.

② Cross into another field and keep to the left-hand side, following the hedgerow, which is now on your left. When you reach the next stile, continue ahead, go past a gate on the left, to reach another stile on the left. Cross this stile and head diagonally right to a stile between the house and the farmyard.

③ Turn left on to the road and walk into the village. Keep left into **Southerndown Road** and then fork right into **Heol-y-slough**. Follow this road for ¾ mile (1.2km) then, as the road bends to the left, keep straight across the common. Continue ahead where a bridleway crosses the track. As you join another track, maintain your direction along the valley floor.

④ The path winds its way down through sand dunes, passing a tributary valley on the left, and eventually emerges on the **B4524**. Cross the road and continue until you locate one of the many paths that lead left towards **Portobello House**. At the drive, keep right, then fork left by the house to continue through the bracken, parallel to the estuary of the **Ogmore River**.

WHERE TO EAT AND DRINK ⓘ
Along the route you'll pass the **Farmers Arms** in St Bride's Major. This is a family orientated pub that does good bar food and also has a separate restaurant (no dogs unfortunately). Another option is a short detour into **Ogmore-by-Sea** where there's plenty of choice from typical beach-side snacks such as chip shops and cafés.

---

⑤ Make sure you stay above the small cliffs near the mouth of estuary and you'll eventually arrive at a **car parking area** above the beach. From here, follow the obvious route along the coast around to the left.

WHILE YOU'RE THERE ⓘ
Only a mile (1.6km) from Ogmore-by-Sea is **Ogmore Castle**, a 12th-century Norman fortification that lies in a pretty green valley and is reputed to be the place where King Arthur was fatally wounded. His body is said to buried in a cave near by. True or not, the ruins, which are very basic but incredibly atmospheric, are well worth a visit.

---

⑥ You'll come to a dry-stone wall, which will funnel you through a gate marked 'Coast Path – Emergency Vehicles Only'. Continue walking along the coast path until, about 1¼ miles (2km) from the gate, you meet with a steep valley. Turn left into this valley and then turn immediately right, on to a footpath that climbs steeply up the grassy hillside.

WHAT TO LOOK FOR ⓘ
If the sea seems a long way out, it's worth remembering that the **tidal flows** in the Bristol Channel are the second largest in the world, with the differences between high and low water being well over 39ft (12m) on a high spring tide. The only larger tides are witnessed in Canada's Bay of Fundy.

---

⑦ Stay with the footpath as it follows the line of a dry-stone wall around to **West Farm**. Keep to the right-hand side of the agricultural buildings and continue to reach the upper car park. A gap in the wall, at the back of this, leads you to a grassy track that follows the road down into **Dunraven**.

Along the Waterfalls

A low-level walk among riverside scenery with four breathtaking waterfalls.

•DISTANCE•	4 miles (6.4km)
•MINIMUM TIME•	2hrs
•ASCENT / GRADIENT•	360ft (110m) ▲▲▲
•LEVEL OF DIFFICULTY•	🚶 🚶 🚶
•PATHS•	Riverside paths, some rough sections and steps, no stiles
•LANDSCAPE•	Wooded valleys, fast flowing rivers, waterfalls
•SUGGESTED MAP•	aqua3 OS Explorer OL12 Brecon Beacons National Park Western & Central areas
•START / FINISH•	Grid reference: SN 928124
•DOG FRIENDLINESS•	Rivers too powerful for fetching sticks
•PARKING•	Park car park at Porth yr ogof, near Ystradfellte
•PUBLIC TOILETS•	At start

BACKGROUND TO THE WALK

In a National Park justly renowned for its sweeping, but barren, mountain scenery, lovers of high ground are in danger of completely overlooking one the Brecon Beacons' hidden gems. This is the pocket of dramatic limestone scenery often referred to as Waterfall Country. South of the upland plateaux of Fforest Fawr, geological faults and water erosion have produced a series of deep, narrow gorges, sheltered by impressive woodland and randomly broken up by a succession of gushing waterfalls. The highlight of this is Sgwd yr Eira, where it's possible to venture right behind the falls. Walking here is a completely different experience to that of the windswept escarpments, but the scenery is marvellous and the generally sheltered nature of the terrain makes it an ideal outing for those days when cloud obscures the peaks.

In simple terms, the falls are the result of a geological fault that pushed the hard sandstone, which makes up the backbone of most of the National Park, up against softer shales. The force of the rivers, which spring up high on the mountains of Fforest Fawr, has eroded the shales leaving shelves of the harder rock exposed. These shelves are clearly visible on most of the waterfalls.

At the southern edge of the high ground, a layer of carboniferous limestone overlies the old red sandstone. This younger rock is soluble in the slightly acidic rain and river water that constantly pounds it. The erosion results in caves like Porth yr ogof at the start of this walk, where the rivers literally disappear underground, and craters where rainwater exploits weaknesses and faults in the rock – these are often referred to as sinkholes or shake holes.

Walk 23 Directions

① Cross the road at the entrance to the car park and head down the left-hand of the two paths, waymarked with a yellow arrow. Follow this path on to the riverbank, then keep the river to your right to follow a rough footpath through a couple of kissing gates to reach a footbridge.

Walk 23

② Continue ahead, drop into a dip and climb steeply out. Keep left to climb to a broken wall where the path forks. Take the left fork here (the bottom right-hand path has a fence along it) and follow the edge of the wood. When you see the odd green-banded marker posts, follow them to a waymarked crossroads where you turn right, now following the red-banded posts.

③ Continue through a dark tunnel of trees and out into more evenly spaced deciduous woodland. Carry on following the waymarked trail to a post directing you downhill. Follow this track, then bear around to the right when you reach the edge of forest. This leads to the top of a set of wooden steps, on the left.

④ Go down the steps to **Sgwd yr Eira** (Waterfall of the Snow) and then, having edged along the bank and walked behind the falls (waterproofs recommended), retrace your steps back to the edge of the wood. Turn left and continue, still following the red-banded posts, to a fork marked with a green-banded post.

⑤ Turn left here and descend to the riverside. Turn left again to **Sgwd y Pannwr** (Fullers Falls), then turn around to walk upstream to **Sgwd Isaf Clun-Gwyn** (Lower Waterfall of the White Meadow). Take care, the ground is very steep and rough around the best viewpoint.

⑥ Retrace your steps downstream to your descent path and turn left to climb back up to the fork at the top. Turn left and follow the red-banded waymarkers along to **Sgwd Clun-gwyn**, where there's a fenced off viewing area. From here, continue along the main trail to the place where you split off earlier.

⑦ Keep to the left-hand side to drop into the dip and retrace your steps past the footbridge and back to **Porth yr ogof**.

And More Hidden Gems

Stunning riverside scenery with a short moorland crossing.
See map and information panel for Walk 23

•DISTANCE•	9½ miles (15.3km)
•MINIMUM TIME•	4hrs 30min
•ASCENT / GRADIENT•	1,180ft (100m) ▲▲▲
•LEVEL OF DIFFICULTY•	🚶🚶🚶

Walk 24 Directions
(Walk 23 option)

At Point ②, cross the footbridge and follow the path upwards until it meets a gravel drive. Turn left and walk out on to the road where you turn right. Pass a small **filling station** on the left and look for a stile on the left. Cross this and walk diagonally across the field to join a walled track.

Keep left on this and walk past a house (**Heol-fawr**) and through a gate. Continue along the track around right- and left-hand bends, then look for a waymarker post showing a permissive path down to the right. Walk down the middle of the field to another post, then down the right-hand edge of a row of trees. Maintain this direction to drop steeply through bracken to a stile above the river.

Turn left and follow the narrow path downstream, crossing a few more stiles as you go. At the road, turn right to cross the bridge and then left into the picnic area of **Pont Melin-fach**, Point Ⓐ. Follow the riverside path past a number of impressive falls and rapids to a wooden footbridge on your left.

Ignore this, but continue to cross another bridge directly ahead. Once over, turn right to follow an easy path to **Sgwd Gwladus** (Waterfall of the Chieftain), Point Ⓑ, then retrace your steps back to the bridge and turn right. Continue along the broad track to the road at **Pontneddfechan**, Point Ⓒ. Turn left to cross the bridge and pass the **White Horse Inn**, then left again on to the road and fork right where the main road goes straight ahead towards Ystradfellte.

Follow the road to a footbridge on the right, cross this and continue to a junction with a broad, hedged track. Turn left on to this and follow it to its end, where you turn left, then right into **Craig y Ddinas** car park. Follow the grassy track up the left-hand side of car park. This turns into a stony path that climbs steeply above the crags.

Continue easily, keeping left at a fork with a track that drops down the fence. At the next fork, keep straight ahead, signposted 'Sgwd yr Eira', and continue along the ridge through a small conifer plantation. This leads to an open grassy area at a junction of paths. Keep ahead to drop steeply down steps to the waterfall at Point ④. Pass beneath the falls and continue with Walk 23.

A Tour of the Castle

An easy saunter through pleasant and varied countryside in the shadow of a spectacular ruin.

•DISTANCE•	4 miles (6.4km)
•MINIMUM TIME•	2hrs
•ASCENT / GRADIENT•	590ft (180m) ▲▲▲
•LEVEL OF DIFFICULTY•	🚶🚶 🚶 🚶
•PATHS•	Good paths and tracks, 17 stiles
•LANDSCAPE•	Rolling pastures and deciduous woodland, short stretches of riverside
•SUGGESTED MAP•	aqua3 OS Explorers OL12 Brecon Beacons National Park Western & Central areas; 178 Llanelli; 186 Llandeilo
•START / FINISH•	Grid reference: SN 666193 (on Explorer OL12)
•DOG FRIENDLINESS•	Not welcome in castle grounds, most stiles not dog friendly, care needed near livestock
•PARKING•	Car park beneath castle
•PUBLIC TOILETS•	At start

Walk 25 Directions

Carreg Cennen is one of the most dramatically positioned castles in the whole of the principality. It occupies an airy perch atop precipitous limestone cliffs and commands fine views in all directions. Throughout this walk you're treated to many fleeting glimpses of the towering spectacle and then at the end you can actually explore the ruins themselves.

From the car park, head out of the gate at the top and proceed towards the castle. As you reach the white building on the right, turn right through a gate on to a footpath. Follow this diagonally leftwards, down to join the fence on the left-hand side of the field and down to a stile that leads on to a road. Turn left and pass a footpath on your right to head around a left-hand bend. Before you reach the house

on the right, turn right over a stile and walk down the centre of the field to another stile. Cross this to drop steeply down to yet another stile and a footbridge across the **River Cennen**.

Cross the bridge and climb steeply up towards the left-hand hedge where you cross an iron gate. Continue upwards, along the hedge, to the top of the field where you bear right to follow it around, beneath **Llwyn-bedw farm**. This leads to an opening in the hedge where you join an obvious farm track and bear right. Follow this across a cattle grid and over a

> **WHILE YOU'RE THERE**
> The colourful Georgian houses and the 19th-century stone bridge, which arches over the River Tywi in a magnificent single span of 145ft (44m), in the market town of **Llandeilo**, make the ancient capital of West Wales a great place to take a look around.

shallow ford to another cattle grid. Climb up a short hill and, at the top, turn left over a stile. Follow the edge of the field to meet a small stream on the right. Continue over a stile and up a stony track, with the stream still on your right, then along the tree-lined path to a stile.

WHERE TO EAT AND DRINK ℹ️

The **café** by the car park is the only place for refreshment on the walk, but this does serve up some great local home-cooked food. If you'd prefer a licensed establishment then head for nearby Trapp, a few miles west of the castle, where the rustic **Cennen Arms** keeps good beer and serves good food.

Cross this, then the adjacent stile by the caving notice, to follow a narrow path down to the source of the **River Loughor**. This is an enchanted spot with the infant river literally gushing to freedom from the cave that has imprisoned it for the formative stages of its life. The limestone landscape in this area of the Black Mountain is peppered with sinkholes and caves similar to this one (► Walk 23). Return to the two stiles and turn right, back on to the footpath, to continue past a lime kiln on the left. Follow the track up and around to the left where it peters out into open pasture. Continue straight ahead to a stile, then bear right, keeping a fenced-off shake hole on the left, to a stile and a narrow road.

Turn left and follow the road up over a cattle grid and around a left-hand bend. As the road swings right, turn left on to a clear farm track. Continue to a fork and keep left to follow a grove of ash trees for 100yds (91m) to a gate and stile on the right. Cross this and head up the narrow field, veering towards the left-hand fence. The views of the castle from here are among the best on the walk. Continue over a stile and along a sunken path to join a stony track. Keep left to a hairpin bend and then turn right, over a stile, to drop to a stream. Bear left on the bank and cross a stile, a footbridge and another stile. This leads to a larger footbridge over the **River Cennen**. Turn right, then left on to a waymarked path that climbs up through oak trees towards the castle.

Carreg Cennen is fairly unique for a Welsh castle in that it was actually built by the Welsh rather than the Normans. The current layout was constructed in the 12th century, although a Roman coin found on the site is evidence of earlier settlement. Despite its seemingly impenetrable location, the castle changed hands numerous times; at one stage it had ten owners in as many years. During the Wars of the Roses in the 15th century, the castle became a den for local bandits and was demolished, brick by brick, to its current condition. Labour was certainly cheap in those days; 500 local men were paid £28 between them to complete the task.

From the entrance, follow the tarmac track down to the car park.

WHAT TO LOOK FOR ℹ️

As you turn from the road into the farm drive at the far end of the walk, the huge banks of earth and rock on the right-hand side are referred to on the map as **Pillow Mounds**. These are thought to be the remains of a Bronze-Age burial site, around 3000 BC, although another line of thought suggests that they could be nothing more sinister than commercially farmed rabbit warrens, a common practice in Victorian times.

Walk 26

The Escarpments of the Carmarthen Fan

An exacting expedition that penetrates some of the Brecon Beacons National Park's most spectacular and remote scenery.

•DISTANCE•	7½ miles (12.1km)
•MINIMUM TIME•	4hrs 30min
•ASCENT / GRADIENT•	2,000ft (610m) ▲▲▲
•LEVEL OF DIFFICULTY•	👥 👥 👥
•PATHS•	Faint paths, trackless sections over open moorland, no stiles
•LANDSCAPE•	Imposing mountains, hidden lakes, wild and remote moorland
•SUGGESTED MAP•	aqua3 OS Explorer OL12 Brecon Beacons National Park Western & Central areas
•START / FINISH•	Grid reference: SN 798238
•DOG FRIENDLINESS•	Care needed near livestock and steep drops
•PARKING•	At end of small unclassified road, south east of Llanddeusant
•PUBLIC TOILETS•	None on route
•NOTE•	Best not undertaken in poor visibility

BACKGROUND TO THE WALK

The view eastwards from the flanks of Bannau Sir Gaer across Llyn y Fan Fach to the steepest section of the Carmarthen Fan is one of my favourites. There's something intangibly special about the broody black waters, their shimmering surface reflecting skywards a rippled mirror image of the impenetrable, shattered crags of the escarpment. Ravens, buzzards and even the occasional red kite ride high on the updraughts and the picture becomes all the more sinister for the addition of a little light cloud, drifting in and out of the summits.

The Lady of the Lake

I'm not the first to become bewitched by this lavish scene. The lake was visited regularly long ago by a local shepherd boy known as Rhiwallon. He encountered a mystical lady, as beautiful as the reflection in the lake that she'd risen from. Her wisdom matched her beauty and she possessed the ability to make healing potions from herbs and flowers. Rhiwallon was captivated, so much so that he proposed marriage and she agreed, but only on the condition that he should never strike her with iron.

Rhiwallon and his wife had a son before the inevitable happened, perhaps by accident, and the lady returned to the dark waters, taking with her all of their worldly goods, including the animals they tended. Fortunately, before she left, she had passed on all of her medicinal skills to her son, who went on to become a local healer. Far fetched? Maybe, but it's perhaps possible to see where the roots of the tale lie. The encroachment of the Iron Age would have certainly been treated with some suspicion by the local population. More interesting, however, is the fact that much later on, the area did actually become renowned for its healers and there followed a long line of successful practitioners known as the Physicians of Myddfai (a small village north of the lake).

The Black Mountain

From the narrow summit of Fan Foel, your grapple with gravity is rewarded by huge views across the bleak uplands of the Black Mountain (singular), not to be confused with the Black Mountains (plural) which are some 30 miles (48km) east of here and visible on a clear day. This is the westernmost mountain range of the National Park and, without doubt, the wildest and most remote. The majority of the land is made up of barren, windswept moorland that possesses an austere beauty with few equals. Unusually, a large percentage is actually owned by the National Park Authority.

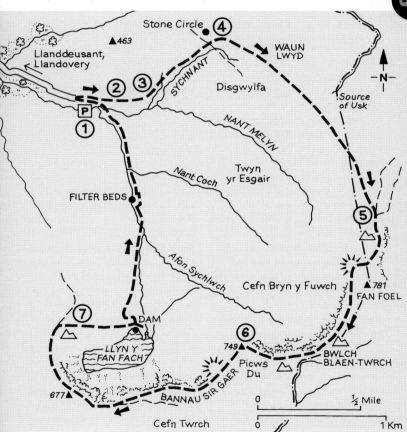

Walk 26 **Directions**

① From the car park at the end of the unclassified road, head back towards Llanddeusant and after about 100yds (91m) turn sharp

right, almost doubling back on yourself, to continue on a faint track that contours eastwards around the hillside. Follow this track as it then veers north east into the small valley carved out by the **Sychnant Brook.**

WHAT TO LOOK FOR

To the south of the escarpment, the old red sandstone which acts as a spine for most of the high ground in the Brecon Beacons, slips beneath a layer of much younger limestone. The distinctive light-coloured outcrops can easily be seen from this walk, especially looking south east from the summit of Bannau Sir Gaer. What aren't so easy to spot are the pot-holes and caves that typify this environment, but if you look at the suggested Ordnance Survey map for this area you will see that it is pockmarked all the way to the Tawe Valley.

② The track becomes clear for a short period, but don't be drawn uphill to the north, instead remain true to the course of the stream, keeping left at the confluence with another distinct valley, this one belonging to the **Nant Melyn**.

③ The track is faint but the going reasonably easy as you continue up the valley, crossing a small tributary and following the bank above the **Sychnant**. Numerous paths and sheep tracks cross your way, but continue unhindered upwards, aiming for the shallow saddle on the blunt ridge above. The stream eventually swings to the right and peters out. At this stage, bear right and head along the ridge.

④ You're now aiming for the steep and obvious spur of **Fan Foel**, which lies south east of you, approximately 1½ miles (2.4km)

away. Follow whatever tracks you can find over **Waun Lwyd** and, as the ridge starts to narrow, keep to the crest where you'll meet a path coming up from the north east.

⑤ Climb steeply up the narrow path on to the escarpment and keep right to follow the escarpment along. The path becomes clearer as it drops steeply into **Bwlch Blaen-Twrch**. From here, climb up on to **Bannau Sir Gaer** and continue to the summit cairn.

WHERE TO EAT AND DRINK

The **Cross Inn** in Llanddeusant is the nearest pub to the start. It's a cosy little place with a roaring log fire and offers a choice of real ales as well as excellent food, including gorgeous local black steak. The pub has also set up a feeding station for local red kites.

⑥ Stay with the main footpath and follow the edge of the escarpment above the precipitous cliffs into a small saddle or col and up again above **Llyn y Fan Fach**. Continue walking, around the lake, with the steep drop to your right-hand side and you'll see a good path dropping down a grassy spur to the outflow of the lake.

⑦ Follow this obvious footpath and then, when you reach the dam, pick up the well-surfaced track that heads back downhill. This will lead you to the right of the waterworks filter beds and back to the car park.

WHILE YOU'RE THERE

The **Dan-yr-Ogof Showcaves**, on the A4067 near Glyntawe, are approximately 10 miles (16.1km) from the start of the walk. Claiming to be the largest cave system in Europe, the huge caverns are certainly spectacular. There are no guided tours, you simply walk yourself around, following a clear path between the stalactites and stalagmites, while listening to a recorded commentary. Other attractions on the site include a dinosaur park, Iron-Age farm, a museum, shire horse centre and a covered children's play area. Open April to September, daily from 10AM, certain days in October.

Take a Walk on the Wild Side

A tough walk, but the only one that really explores the more austere side of the Welsh uplands.

•DISTANCE•	9½ miles (15.3km)
•MINIMUM TIME•	6hrs
•ASCENT / GRADIENT•	2,000ft (610m) ▲▲ ▲▲ ▲
•LEVEL OF DIFFICULTY•	🚶🚶 🚶🚶 🚶🚶
•PATHS•	Riverside path, faint or non-existent paths over moorland, some good tracks, 4 stiles
•LANDSCAPE•	Stunning valley, remote moorland, some forestry
•SUGGESTED MAP•	aqua3 OS Explorer 200 Llandrindod Wells & Elan Valley
•START / FINISH•	Grid reference: SN 863533
•DOG FRIENDLINESS•	Care needed near livestock
•PARKING•	Lay-by on minor road by bridge over Afon Gwesyn or by WC ¼ mile (400m) to south west (grid ref SN 859861)
•PUBLIC TOILETS•	At car park near start
•NOTE•	Avoid in poor visibility

BACKGROUND TO THE WALK

This is the toughest walk in the whole book, but more by the nature of the terrain than the amount of ascent. The rewards, for those who are prepared to navigate their way carefully over one short stretch of trackless moorland, are rich beyond description, for this is a foray into the wilder side of Wales – a place that sees few footprints. For less experienced walkers, this is definitely one to tackle only after you've cut your teeth on the high ground of the Brecon Beacons, and then only in good visibility. Alternatively, if you're unsure about the navigation, or if you are in any doubt about the visibility, follow the outward leg on to Drygarn Fawr and return by retracing your steps.

The Red Kite
The remote nature of the landscape links this area, more than any other, with one of Britain's most beautiful birds, the red kite. It was the scene of this most majestic raptor's final stand. Free of persecution, pesticides and disturbance, a mere handful defiantly resisted extinction by scavenging these moors and nesting in the abundance of trees that line the valleys. Their decline was thankfully halted by a number of conservation groups who, working closely with local landowners, started a release programme of birds imported from Scandinavia and Spain. Successful breeding in both England and Scotland began in 1992 and since then the population has increased significantly.

The birds are easily distinguished from the more common buzzard, which can also be seen in this area, as they are much slimmer in build with narrower, more angular wings and a distinct fork in the longer tail. The plumage is a mixture of russet red and chestnut brown with white wing patches and a silver head. Their flight is more agile and a close view will show the tail constantly twisting as if trimming a sail.

Walk 27

Walk 27 Directions

① Head up the gravel track west of the lay-by and turn right, through a gate. Follow the track across fields and down to the **Afon Gwesyn**, which you ford. Continue to a gate and up towards a wood where the track splits. Choose the top option and then, as this bends around to the left and heads downhill, fork right, to traverse the clearing to a gap in the wood.

Walk 27

② Follow the path down to a ford. Climb on to open ground and bear right to a farm track by some buildings. Turn left on to this and follow it through a gate and beneath some crags. Ignore a fork to the left and continue to open ground. Follow the east side of the valley for over 1½ miles (2.4km) to a **waterfall**.

③ Pass this on the right, then continue until the path almost disappears. Follow the line of the stream until you reach a distinctive small ridge coming in from the right. Take this for 100yds (91m) and bear left on to a narrow path, which leads you around a number of boggy patches until the cairned summit of **Drygarn Fawr** becomes visible ahead.

> **WHERE TO EAT AND DRINK** ⓘ
> The **Neuadd Arms** in Llanwrtyd Wells is a haven for walkers and an excellent pub with a good atmosphere, a glowing fire and tasty food. Dogs allowed in the bar.

④ Climb the grassy slope to the trig point, then follow the ridge east past both **cairns**. A close scan of the hillsides to the south east should reveal two grassy tops, 1½ miles (2.4km) away, one with a large cairn on top – this is **Carnau**, your next objective. A clear grassy track descends east from the cairn. Follow this until it levels completely and rounds a left-hand bend, where you'll make out a faint path forking right. This is the start of the careful navigation and if you're in any doubt about visibility, you'll be better off turning around and retracing your tracks.

⑤ Follow the track, which links a number of boundary stones for 200yds (183m), until you see one

stone offset to the right of the path. Turn sharp right here (south), away from the path, and cross wet ground to climb slightly on to a very broad rounded ridge. You'll make out the head of a small valley ahead and, as you drop into this, bear slightly left to follow the high ground with the valley to your right. Continue on sheep tracks to cross a couple of hollows, until you reach a grassy hilltop. From here, you should be able to see the cairn ahead. Take the clear path that leads to it.

⑥ From **Carnau** you'll see the start of a clear gorge away to the south west. Walk towards this and pick up a good track that leads across the river. Follow the bank to the left to reach a fork and then take the right-hand path to descend open hillsides and drop into the bottom of the valley, where it meets the wood.

⑦ Go through the gate and follow the forest track down across a stream and up to a five-way junction. Turn sharp right here, go through a gate and then another on the left. Drop down through the field on to an enclosed track and follow this to a junction above some houses on your left. Keep right, cross a stream and then take the track across a field to a path junction. Keep straight ahead and descend past **Glangwesyn** to the road. Turn right on to the road to return to your car.

> **WHILE YOU'RE THERE** ⓘ
> In winter, enquire in the Neuadd Arms in Llanwrtyd Wells for details of the **red kite feeding** which usually takes place at around 12:30PM near a hide on the outskirts of the village. It can be quite spectacular and will guarantee you a sighting of these wonderful birds.

Back to Nature

The formidable crags of one of the Beacon's best-known nature reserves.

•DISTANCE•	4 miles (6.4km)
•MINIMUM TIME•	2hrs
•ASCENT / GRADIENT•	1,050ft (320m) ▲▲▲
•LEVEL OF DIFFICULTY•	🚶🚶 🚶🚶 🚶
•PATHS•	Clear footpaths and broad stony tracks, 4 stiles
•LANDSCAPE•	Imposing crags and rolling moorland, great views
•SUGGESTED MAP•	aqua3 OS Explorer OL12 Brecon Beacons National Park Western & Central areas
•START / FINISH•	Grid reference: SN 972221
•DOG FRIENDLINESS•	Difficult stiles, care near livestock, on lead in nature reserve
•PARKING•	Pull-in by small picnic area on A470, 2 miles (3.2km) north of Storey Arms
•PUBLIC TOILETS•	Storey Arms car park

BACKGROUND TO THE WALK

This is a short walk but it has much to offer. Firstly, there are some fine views over the Tarell Valley to the true kings of the National Park, Pen y Fan and Corn Du, whose lofty crowns command your attention for most of the way round. And secondly, the daunting crags of Craig Cerrig-gleisiad are a true spectacle in their own right and are well worth admiring close up, both from below and above.

This is a unique environment and, as such, it hosts a range of habitats that support a number of rare species of flora and fauna. The cirque itself was formed by the action of an ice-age glacier, which scoured out a deep hollow in the hillside and then deposited the rocks it had accumulated at the foot of the cliff to form banks of moraine. The retreating ice left a legacy – a selection of arctic-alpine plants that were sheltered from the rising temperatures by the north-facing escarpment. These plants, which include saxifrages and roseroot, also need a lime-rich soil, present on the escarpments but not on the more acidic moorland on the tops. For most of these plants, the Brecon Beacons represent the southernmost part of their range.

The cliffs only make up a fraction of the 156-acre (63ha) National Nature Reserve. One of the things that makes Craig Cerrig-gleisiad – which means 'Blue-stone Rock' – special is the diversity of the terrain. The lower slopes are home to mixed woodland and flowers such as orchids and anemones, while the high ground supports heather and bilberry. You'll see plenty of sheep within the reserve, but grazing is controlled to ensure a variety of habitats. The diversity isn't just restricted to plants either – 16 species of butterfly have been recorded on the reserve and over 80 different types of birds, including the ring ouzel, or mountain blackbird as it's often known, and the peregrine falcon, which is definitely a bird of the cliffs.

This mainly upland region of the Brecon Beacons National Park is partitioned from the central Brecon Beacons by the deep slash of the Taf and Tarell valleys. The name Fforest Fawr, which means Great Forest, comes not from trees but from its one-time status as a royal hunting ground. The high ground is largely untracked and barren, but the north-facing escarpment, of which Craig Cerrig-gleisiad forms a part, is steep and impressive. As the land

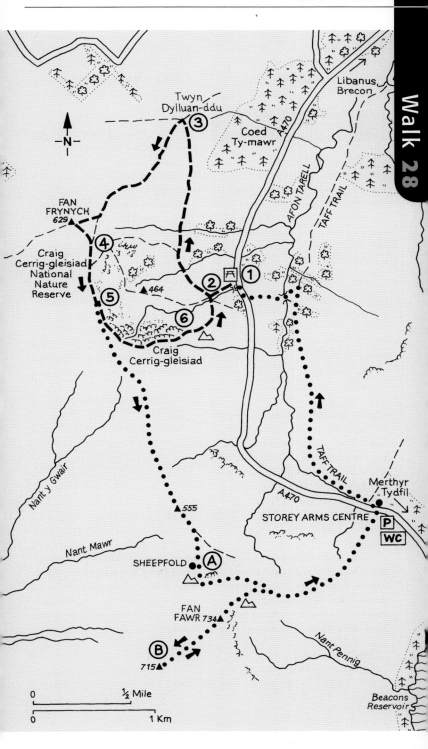

Walk 28

dips to the south, it is chiselled into a succession of north–south running valleys that cradle the infant forms of some of the National Park's greatest rivers. These are seen to best effect on the southern fringes of the park, where they form Fforest Fawr's greatest spectacle, Waterfall Country (► Walk 23).

Walk 28 Directions

① There's a bridge and a small picnic area at the southern end of the lay-by. Walk towards this and go through the adjacent kissing gate (signposted to Twyn Dylluan-ddu and Forest Lodge). Head towards the crags, following a clear footpath, until you come to a gap in the next wall.

WHILE YOU'RE THERE

This is the nearest walk to the **National Park Visitor Centre** on Mynydd Illtud Common, near Libanus. It's a great source of information about the National Park, hosts some great displays and has a programme of guided walks.

---

② Pass through this and turn right to follow a dry-stone wall north. Head down into a small valley, cross the stream, then a stile to continue in the same direction. Drop into another, steeper, valley and climb out, still following the track. Continue through the bracken to a stile.

③ Cross and turn left on to a stony track. Follow this up to a gate and a stile and continue through rough ground, churned up by mining, until it levels on a dished plateau. Bear right here to the whitewashed

trig point of **Fan Frynych**, then turn sharp left to return to the main track above the escarpment.

④ Turn right on to the main track again and continue past more rough ground before dropping slightly into a broad but shallow valley. At the bottom, go over a stile by a gate.

⑤ Cross another stile on your left and turn right to continue in the same direction, this time with the fence to your right. Climb up to the highest point, then follow the obvious path around the top of the cliffs. The path starts to drop, easily at first but getting steeper as you go.

WHERE TO EAT AND DRINK

The **National Park Visitor Centre** at Libanus serves tasty lunches, with vegetarian options, as well as delicious home-made cakes. If you fancy a pub there's the **Tai'r Bull Inn**, also at Libanus (► Where To Eat and Drink, Walk 30).

---

⑥ Continue carefully down the steep section and follow the path around to the left when you reach easier ground. This leads you to a stream, which you can ford or jump (it's narrower a few paces downstream). Turn right, through the gap in the wall, and follow the outward path back to the car park.

WHAT TO LOOK FOR

Much of the outward leg follows the line of a pristine **dry-stone wall**. Although changes in farming practices in the hills haven't altered as radically as they have in many lowland areas, the hedgerows and walls that once divided the land are expensive to maintain and have been slowly replaced by wire fences. The National Park Authority provides free consultation to landowners wishing to keep the more scenic traditional crafts alive.

And on into Fforest Fawr

Extend Walk 28 to the highest peak in the range.
See map and information panel for Walk 28

•DISTANCE•	8 miles (12.9km)
•MINIMUM TIME•	5hrs
•ASCENT / GRADIENT•	1,600ft (488m) ▲▲▲
•LEVEL OF DIFFICULTY•	🚶🚶🚶

Walk 29 Directions (Walk 28 option)

The untracked moorland of Fforest Fawr sees far fewer visitors than the mountains on the other side of the main thoroughfare. For this reason, it's always refreshing to escape the crowds and climb the highest, and easiest to access, mountain in the range, Fan Fawr. The route across the tops from Craig Cerrig-gleisiad is a good introduction to the type of walking found in this area.

Leave Walk 28 at Point ⑤ and climb out of the valley, following the fence on your left, until you see your next objective, **Fan Fawr**, looming large ahead. Between you and its rounded summit lies a few miles of open moorland that typifies this part of the National Park. Head uphill to the pile of stones that mark the summit of **Craig Cerrig-gleisiad**, then follow a faint path that runs along the ridge towards the peak.

As the path starts to drop, look for a faint track that forks right. Follow this towards a small crag on the steep hillside, at the same height as you are. You'll pass a circular sheepfold, Point Ⓐ, before climbing steeply up the grassy bank to the right of the small crag until you come to a slim terrace that contours around the hillside. Turn left on to this and walk around the eastern flank of the mountain until you eventually meet the well-trodden main track, coming up from your left. Turn right on to this and follow it steeply to the top. Continue south west to the trig point, Point Ⓑ, and then retrace your steps back to the steep path. Drop down and continue into a boggy saddle, where the path becomes harder to follow. Maintain the same direction, climbing slightly to leave the saddle, then drop easily down to a stile in the car park on the **A470**.

Cross the road to the **Storey Arms** and turn left. You'll see a track that forks off to the right (signposted 'Taff Trail'). This is the line of the old road that ran between Merthyr Tydfil and Brecon. In those days the Storey Arms was a coaching inn. Follow this through a couple of bands of woodland to a waymarked footpath on the left, in the corner of a wood. Take this and drop down to a footbridge that crosses the **Afon Tarell**. Climb up the opposite bank and keep straight ahead to pass a large oak tree and meet the **A470** again, at a stile. Turn right to return to the car park at Point ①.

Walk 30

The Pen y Fan Pilgrimage – a Circular Route

A straightforward circuit that follows the main trade routes up on to the roof of the National Park.

•DISTANCE•	5 miles (8km)
•MINIMUM TIME•	2hrs 30min
•ASCENT / GRADIENT•	1,610ft (491m) ▲▲▲
•LEVEL OF DIFFICULTY•	🚶🚶 🚶🚶 🚶
•PATHS•	Clearly defined tracks, 2 stiles
•LANDSCAPE•	Rugged high mountains and deeply scooped valleys
•SUGGESTED MAP•	aqua3 OS Explorer OL12 Brecon Beacons National Park Western & Central areas
•START / FINISH•	Grid reference: SN 982203
•DOG FRIENDLINESS•	Care needed near sheep and on cliff tops
•PARKING•	Lay-by on A470, opposite Storey Arms and telephone box
•PUBLIC TOILETS•	¼ mile (400m) south of start

Walk 30 Directions

Every mountain has its 'trade route' – the easiest and most trafficked way to the top – and Pen y Fan is no different. This is the highest peak in southern Britain and the closest real mountain to a huge chunk of the population, attracting mass pilgrimages from the Home Counties, Birmingham, Bristol and South Wales. The most commonly used tactic is an out-and-back approach, using the motorway-like track that heads west from the southern edge of the small plantation, but this is less rewarding than the simple circular route described here, which starts by crossing the head of the Taff Valley.

Cross the road and the stile next to the **telephone box**. The large building to your right is the **Storey Arms**, now an outdoor education centre but once a wayside inn on the coaching road between Brecon and South Wales. The original road can be seen forking off to your left, this forms a section of the Taff Trail, a long distance route between Cardiff and Brecon (➤ Walk 41). Follow a clear, in places artificial, path up the hillside, leaving the plantation behind and crossing the open moorland of the southern flanks of **Y Gyrn** – a rounded summit to your left. You'll soon gain the ridge and cross a stile to drop easily down to the infant **Taf Fawr** – a pleasant and sheltered spot, ideal for a break before you reach the exposed hilltops above. The way ahead is clear, with the rough and badly eroded track climbing steeply up the hillside opposite. Follow this until it reaches the escarpment edge above the magnificent valley of **Cwm Llwch**. Below you'll see the glacier-formed lake of Llyn Cwm Llwch, and above this the steep head wall that unites the twin peaks.

Turn right to follow the clear path up towards the rocky ramparts of **Corn Du**. The path slips easily around the craggy outcrops and leads you up to the huge cairn on top of the broad summit plateau. The views down the valley are awesome, but take care as some of the summit rocks pretty much overhang the chasm below.

The way to **Pen y Fan** is obvious from here. Drop into the shallow saddle to the east and continue easily on to the summit. This opens up a whole new vista, with the narrow ridge of **Cefn Cwm Llwch** acting as the dividing wall for the remote **Cwm Sere**, to the right as you look out.

The north east face of the mountain is particularly precipitous so take care near the edges. The most enjoyable way to begin your descent is to retrace your steps across Corn Du to **Bwlch Duwynt**, the obvious saddle between the summit and the long ridge that runs south. Alternatively, a good path runs below Corn Du, allowing easy passage with no extra height gain. To locate this, drop back into the saddle you've just crossed and fork left, beneath the grassy slope that leads to the summit. The views from this section are to the south, over the two Neuadd reservoirs.

Bwlch Duwynt represents a fairly major junction of paths, but you'll easily locate the main track that leads downhill to your right, away from Corn Du. Again, sections of this track have been laid in stone in recent years to restrict the erosion caused by thousands of walkers' feet. Follow the track easily down for just over a mile (1.6km) until you see the **Taf Fawr** river to your right-hand side.

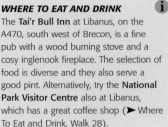

WHERE TO EAT AND DRINK

The **Tai'r Bull Inn** at Libanus, on the A470, south west of Brecon, is a fine pub with a wood burning stove and a cosy inglenook fireplace. The selection of food is diverse and they also serve a good pint. Alternatively, try the **National Park Visitor Centre** also at Libanus, which has a great coffee shop (► Where To Eat and Drink, Walk 28).

A short diversion to your right just here will reveal a great, rocky picnic spot, situated above a small waterfall. Continue down to ford the river and go through the kissing gate into the main car park. Turn right into the car park and follow it to its end where a gravel footpath (signposted with a **Taff Trail** waymarker) takes over.

Continue along the side of the **plantation** and cross the road to return to the start.

WHILE YOU'RE THERE

Looking north from Pen y Fan, you'll see **Brecon**, tucked away at the foot of the mountains. It's the largest town in the National Park and also the administrative centre of the park authority. Brecon grew up as a walled settlement surrounding an 11th-century Norman castle and a Benedictine priory, which later formed part of the impressive Brecon Cathedral. It saw its steepest growth at the start of the Industrial Revolution, when it was linked with the ports to the south by a canal and railway line. Once the county town of Brecknockshire, these days Brecon relies on tourism and agriculture for most of its income. It makes a great base for exploring the National Park and has plenty of attractions in its own right. In addition to the cathedral, there's a county museum, a military museum and a theatre.

Walk 31

The Brecon Beacons from the Neuadd Reservoirs

A magical tour of reservoirs, high ridges and the highest mountains in southern Britain.

•DISTANCE•	7½ miles (12.1km)
•MINIMUM TIME•	4hrs
•ASCENT / GRADIENT•	2,000ft (610m) ▲▲▲
•LEVEL OF DIFFICULTY•	🚶🚶 🚶
•PATHS•	Clear well-trodden paths, small boggy patches, broad rocky track, 1 stile
•LANDSCAPE•	Steep rocky escarpments overlooking deep U-shaped valley and two small reservoirs
•SUGGESTED MAP•	aqua3 OS Explorer OL12 Brecon Beacons National Park Western & Central areas
•START / FINISH•	Grid reference: SO 032179
•DOG FRIENDLINESS•	Care needed near livestock, several steep drops
•PARKING•	At end of small lane leading north from Pontsticill
•PUBLIC TOILETS•	None on route

BACKGROUND TO THE WALK

This is a fine way to visit the area's highest ground, particularly if you feel like a longer outing than Walk 30 but are afraid of over-committing yourself, as any, or all, of the big peaks can be by-passed if required. It's also an easy way to gain the tops, as it starts at an altitude over 1,300ft (396m) and, with the exception of two short but stiff sections, the climbing remains gentle to the point of being almost undetectable.

Beautiful Valley

The Taf Fechan has certainly carved itself a beautiful valley. Its grand sweeping architecture doesn't appear any the worse for the addition of the two Neuadd reservoirs. The lower reservoir, nearest the start, opened in 1884 to provide water for Merthyr Tydfil, which during the early days of the Industrial Revolution had become something of a boom town. As the iron and steel production increased, and with it the local population, demand started to outstrip supply and the valley was dammed again, this time higher up.

High Peaks

Once up, the walk cruises easily along the sandstone promenade of Graig Fan Ddu and Craig Gwaun Taf, offering great views across the magnificent cwm to the steep head of the valley, where the two highest peaks in southern Britain preside. It also rewards the walker with some tantalising glimpses of the stunning and seldom visited valley of Cwm Crew, which runs south west from the narrowest section of the ridge at Rhiw yr Ysgyfarnog – the Slope of the Hare. The high peaks need little introduction. Their might and stature are clear from almost any viewpoint, although you may find yourself surprised by the sheer scale of the drop from the north face of Corn Du and the incomparable north east face of Pen y Fan, which falls precipitously down over 1,000ft (305m) to the rolling moorland of Cwm Sere below. Not so surprising are the views from the top which, as you'd expect, are magnificent and matched only by the elation of reaching the summit. Incidentally, the correct pronunciation of the peak's name is 'van'; the 'f' is pronounced as a 'v' in Welsh. As you'd expect, the highest peaks also act as a divide for the watersheds, with the water to the north draining into the Usk and the hills to the south feeding the Taff, which runs south to Cardiff.

To an Ancient Track

Steep and rocky ground leads down from the table-top summit, with the grassy flanks of Cribyn appearing much steeper than they really are up ahead. If you don't think you can manage another climb, sneak around the peak to the right, otherwise, more fine views await you on the cramped summit. This time you can gaze north over Cwm Cynwyn, as fine a natural amphitheatre as you're ever likely to see. With the peaks bagged, you'll drop into the atmospheric rocky saddle of Bwlch ar y Fan and pick up an ancient track, known locally as the 'Gap Road'. Although many claim it be of Roman origin, the exact age of the track isn't known. It does however, afford easy progress for tired legs back down to the reservoirs. The grassy shores of the lower lake make a great sun-trap and an excellent picnic spot from where you can look back up the valley to the impressive outlines of the mountains you've just climbed.

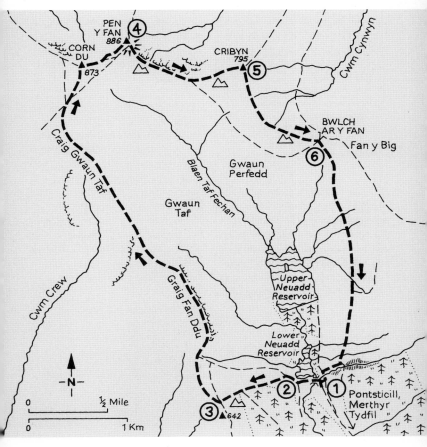

Walk 31

Walk 31 Directions

① Continue up the lane to a small gate, which leads into the grounds of the reservoir. Keep walking straight ahead to drop down a narrow path to a concrete bridge across an outflow. Cross the bridge and climb up on to the bank opposite where you bear left to walk along the top of the bank. This will take you to a gate that leads out on to open moorland.

② Go through this and keep straight ahead, taking the left-hand of the two tracks, which leads easily uphill towards the edge of a mainly felled forest. Follow the clear track up, with the forest to your left, and then climb steeply up a stony gully to the top of the escarpment.

> **WHAT TO LOOK FOR** ⓘ
> The summits of Pen y Fan, Corn Du and Cribyn were once all crowned with Bronze-Age **burial cairns**, probably dating back to around 1800 BC. It's clear that the mountains held some significance, even way back then.

③ Once there, turn right on to the obvious path and follow the escarpment along for over 2½ miles (4km). You'll eventually drop into a distinct saddle with the flat-topped summit of **Corn Du** directly ahead. Where the path forks, keep straight ahead and climb easily up on to the summit. Follow the escarpment edge along and then drop down into another saddle, where you take the path up on to the next peak, **Pen y Fan**.

④ Again, from the summit cairn, follow the escarpment around and drop steeply, on a rocky path, down into a deep col beneath **Cribyn**. Keep straight ahead to climb steeply up to the cairn on the narrow summit. Note: this climb can be avoided by forking right and following another clear path that contours right around the southern flanks of the mountain and brings you out at Point ⑥.

⑤ From the top, bear slightly right and follow the escarpment around to the south east. After a long flat stretch, you'll drop steeply down into to a deep col known as **Bwlch ar y Fan**.

⑥ Cross the stile and turn right on to the well-made track that leads easily down the mountain. Follow this for over 1½ miles (2.4km), until it starts to swing slightly to the left and drops steeply into a rocky ravine. Turn right here on to a track and take it down to a gate. Go through this, turn left and follow the track to its end. Turn right on to another track that leads back to the head of the lane. Go through the gate and follow the lane back.

> **WHILE YOU'RE THERE** ⓘ
> Head south to Pant, north of Merthyr Tydfil, and take a ride aboard the **Brecon Mountain Railway**, a narrow-gauge steam train that takes a 50-minute return trip along the side of the Taf Fechan Reservoir to Dol-y-Gaer. It is great scenery and lots of fun. Open from April to October.

> **WHERE TO EAT AND DRINK**
> The most popular pubs in the area are at nearby Talybont-on-Usk (follow the narrow lane past the beautiful Talybont Reservoir), where the pick of the bunch is the **Traveller's Rest**, on the outskirts of the village towards Llangynidr. This has a delightful canal-side garden and a good restaurant. There's also a pleasant **tea shop** in the village.

Tragedy and Spectacle on the Beacons Horseshoe

Take the connoisseur's way to the highest ground in southern Britain.

•DISTANCE•	7 miles (11.3km)
•MINIMUM TIME•	4hrs
•ASCENT / GRADIENT•	2,100ft (640m) ▲▲▲
•LEVEL OF DIFFICULTY•	🚶 🚶 🚶
•PATHS•	Well-defined paths and tracks, short distance on quiet lanes, 4 stiles
•LANDSCAPE•	Lofty peaks, angular ridges and magnificent valleys
•SUGGESTED MAP•	aqua3 OS Explorer OL12 Brecon Beacons National Park Western & Central areas
•START / FINISH•	Grid reference: SO 025248
•DOG FRIENDLINESS•	Care needed near sheep, some steep cliffs
•PARKING•	Car park at end of small lane, 3 miles (4.8km) south of Brecon
•PUBLIC TOILETS•	None on route

BACKGROUND TO THE WALK

Few stories tear at the heartstrings quite as much as the tragic tale of Tommy Jones. In August 1900 the five-year-old and his father were walking from the railway station in Brecon to his grandfather's farm in Cwm Llwch. They rested a while at the army camp at Login where Tommy's grandfather and his 13-year-old cousin, Willie, met them. The two men decided to stay a while with the soldiers but the two boys continued on to the farmhouse, ½ mile (800m) away. As darkness fell, Tommy got scared. Willie wanted to continue to the farmhouse, but Tommy decided to return to his father. Sadly, he never made it. Willie rejoined the men shortly and, realising that the boy had vanished, a huge search ensued. The scale of the search increased as the days went by. There were even suggestions that he'd been kidnapped or murdered. Remarkably, a few weeks later, a local woman dreamt about the boy and, although she had never been there before, was able to lead her husband up on to the ridge where they discovered Tommy's remains. A simple stone obelisk was erected close to the spot where the body was found. It was moved slightly in 1997, as the area surrounding it had become badly eroded.

Spectacular Route

This is far and away the most spectacular route up on to the highest ground of the National Park. The jagged ridges, steep gullies and deeply gouged valleys pay more than a passing resemblance to those of the higher mountains of Snowdonia, many miles further north. It's only the popularity of the peaks, which are easily reached from the road (► Walk 30), which prevents it from feeling like a really wild day out in the mountains. The biggest climb comes early on, with a steep pull up from the car park on to the head of the lovely and remote Cwm Gwdi. The path then follows rocky, disused quarry tracks for the most part, before finally hurdling the grassy spur that leads on to Cefn Cwm Llwch.

The ridge is by no means knife-edge, but it does feel incredibly airy, dividing two magnificent valleys, both cradling fast-flowing mountain streams. The rocky ramparts of the summit seem to taunt you as you continue southwards and then, as you reach the steep final step, the spectacular north east face of Pen y Fan presents itself in its full glory. This is probably the most magnificent section of mountain scenery in the whole National Park. Steep gullies drop down from the summit, vaulting vertical crags as they plummet into the valley below, and ravens play on the ever-present updraughts.

The summit, often crowded, can come as an anti-climax after the wild scenery you've just witnessed, but it's a great mountain and there's plenty more on the descent from Corn Du. After crossing the void between the peaks, you'll trace the airy tops of Craig Cwm Llwch past the Tommy Jones obelisk, one of the Beacons' best-known landmarks. You'll then drop to a fine example of a glacial lake, Llyn Cwm Llwch, which makes an excellent picnic spot, surrounded still by the formidable walls of the head of the valley.

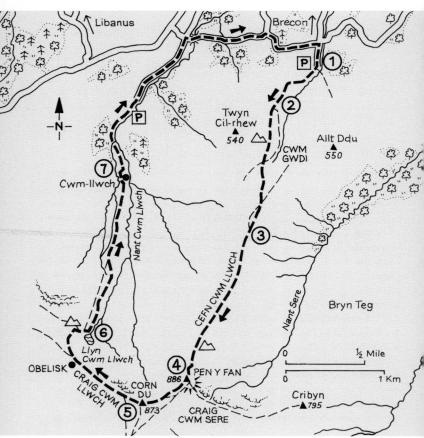

Walk 32 Directions

① Walk uphill from the car park and pass an information plinth

before crossing a stile. Walk along the right-hand side of the field to the top right-hand corner and then bear left to continue along the fence to another stile.

WHAT TO LOOK FOR

As you descend from the escarpment into Cwm Llwch, you'll drop to the shores of **Llyn Cwm Llwch**, a fine example of a mountain lake left behind the last ice age. As the glaciers that shaped the head of the valley retreated, the rocks and stones that they had scoured from the steep slopes were deposited at their feet creating a wall, or bank, known as moraine. This effectively creates a dam for the lake to form.

② Follow the broad but faint grassy track straight on. It gradually becomes a better-defined stony track that swings slightly left and climbs the hillside. Continue ahead, up towards the head of **Cwm Gwdi**, and keep ahead, ignoring a few right forks, until the path eventually levels out on **Cefn Cwm Llwch**.

WHERE TO EAT AND DRINK

There's nothing close to the walk, but Brecon has plenty of choice including the scruffy but excellent value **Three Horseshoes** on Bridge Street, and **Roberto's**, a cosy Mediterranean eatery near the centre. Alternatively, for a cuppa and a cake, try the **National Park Visitor Centre** near Libanus (➤ Where To Eat and Drink, Walk 28).

③ Continue along the ridge towards the summit ahead. As you reach the foot of the peak, the track steepens considerably, offering a fine viewpoint over a perilous gully that drops into **Cwm Sere** on the left. Continue to climb steeply over a few rocky steps to reach the summit cairn on **Pen y Fan**.

④ Bear right to follow the escarpment edge along and drop into a shallow saddle beneath the rising crest of **Corn Du**. Continue up on to this summit, then bear left to drop down through rocky outcrops on to easier ground below. Bear sharp right once you reach the grassy hillside to walk north beneath the peak.

⑤ Continue down the hill and pass the **Tommy Jones obelisk** (➤ Background to the Walk) with the steep crags of Craig Cwm Llwch on your right-hand side. Above the lake, the path forks; take the right-hand option and drop steeply, around a dog-leg and over moraine banks to the lake shore.

⑥ A clear track leads north from the lake; follow it over easy ground to cross a wall that leads on to a broad farm track. Take this down to a gate in front of a building and climb the stile on the left. Cross the compound and climb another stile to follow waymarker posts around to the right on to another track, beyond the building.

⑦ Bear left on to this track and follow it down, over a footbridge, to a parking area. Keep straight ahead, through a gate to a T-junction, where you turn right. Cross the bridge and continue for over a mile (1.6km) to another T-junction. Turn right and walk uphill back to the car park.

WHILE YOU'RE THERE

Hidden beneath a poverty stricken and somewhat dowdy reputation, **Merthyr Tydfil** is one of South Wales most fascinating towns – even its name, which was derived from the story of Tydfil, a martyred Welsh Princess, is full of intrigue. The town's hey-day came during the Industrial Revolution when it was the most populated town in Wales. It now boasts a great museum in the shape of Cyfartha Castle, which will certainly shed some light on a chequered and often bloody past.

Walk 33

Skyline Walking Above the Caerfanell Valley

Spectacular escarpments above a wild and remote valley that shelters a touching memorial.

•DISTANCE•	5½ miles (8.8km)
•MINIMUM TIME•	3hrs 30min
•ASCENT / GRADIENT•	1,542ft (470m) ▲▲▲
•LEVEL OF DIFFICULTY•	🚶 🚶 🚶
•PATHS•	Clear tracks across open mountain tops, along river and through forest, some mud and wet peat, 3 stiles
•LANDSCAPE•	Moorland, craggy escarpments, remote valley, coniferous plantation, waterfalls
•SUGGESTED MAP•	aqua3 OS Explorer OL12 Brecon Beacons National Park Western & Central areas
•START / FINISH•	Grid reference: SO 056175
•DOG FRIENDLINESS•	Care needed near livestock, 1 dog-proof stile
•PARKING•	Large car park at start, 3 miles (4.8km) west of Talybont Reservoir
•PUBLIC TOILETS•	None on route

BACKGROUND TO THE WALK

If I were asked to recommend just one walk that summed up everything good about walking in the Brecon Beacons, it would be this one. In only 5½ miles (8.8km), it encapsulates almost every sort of landscape found in the National Park.

High Mountain Scenery

It starts by climbing steeply on to an impressive peak from where you track easily along a steep sandstone escarpment, so typical of the area's high mountain scenery. The airy path crosses the head of a precipitous waterfall, rubs shoulders with an expansive moorland plateau and provides views that will remain in your memory for a long time. At the half-way stage, you'll get a sneak peep of the highest peaks in the National Park as well as a bird's-eye view over Cwm Oergwm, one of the most spectacular valleys in a wild land that's famed for them. The return leg passes the forlorn wreckage of a Canadian warplane and a fitting memorial to those who perished in her, before dropping easily down to follow a delightful upland river past a series of tumbling waterfalls. It finishes with a steep pull up through a small plantation, bejewelled by further cascades and rapids.

Death Flight

As you approach the clearly visible cairn beneath Waun Rydd, a sharp eye will spot flashes of red, draped over the impeccable stonework. As you draw closer, you'll see that the red is in fact, a plethora of poppy wreaths hung over a simple memorial. A bronze plaque lists the names of the young Canadians who lost their lives when Wellington bomber R1645 came down in bad weather, following a routine training flight on 6 July 1942. The twisted wreckage, a deathly shade of dull grey, lies strewn around the bracken covered hillside below the cairn. The serenity and beauty of the Beacons' landscape makes a fitting backdrop to the scene and it's always difficult to pass this spot without pausing for reflection.

Cwar y Gigfran

Gigfran is Welsh for raven and the diminutive crag that shades the memorial is named after these powerful birds that can often be seen performing aerobatics above it. They are the largest members of the corvid family, easily distinguished from carrion crows, rooks, jackdaws and the rarer chough, by their size. Ravens are synonymous with remote upland areas and rugged coastal regions, where they tend to nest on crags and perform tumbling flight displays that appear more for pleasure than for purpose. Although the majority of their nourishment in the mountain environment comes from sheep carrion, they are endlessly resourceful and incredibly skilful hunters too.

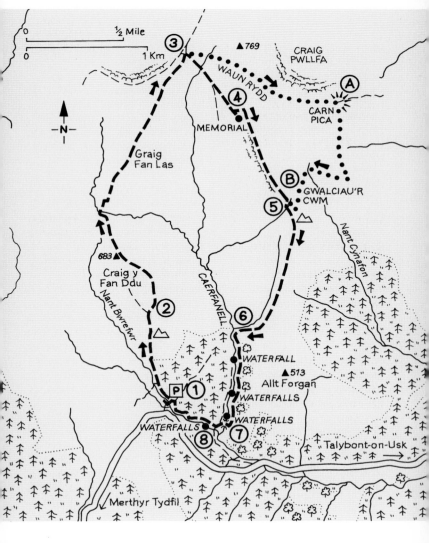

Walk 33

Walk 33 Directions

① Walk back out of the car park, either crossing the cattle grid or a stile to the left, then turn immediately right on to a stone track that heads uphill, with the stream on your left. Follow this track steeply up to the top of the escarpment and keep straight ahead to cross the narrow spur, where you bear around, slightly to the left, to follow the escarpment.

② Stay on the clear path, with the escarpment to your right, for about 1½ miles (2.4km), till you meet a number of paths at the head of the valley.

WHERE TO EAT AND DRINK ⓘ

There's a tea shop in the **post office** at Talybont-on-Usk, as well as four pubs in the village. The best of these is the **Traveller's Rest**, 500yds (457m) south east of the village on the road to Llangynidr. It has a canal-side garden and a good restaurant.

---

③ Take the sharp right turn to follow a narrow track slightly downwards, around the head of the valley, towards the cliffs that can be seen on the opposite hillside. Keep left at a fork and continue to the crash **memorial**.

④ Almost directly above the memorial, you'll see a rocky gully leading up on to the ridge. On the left-hand side of this, as you look at it, is a faint track that climbs steeply up. Take this to the top and turn right on to a narrow but clear track. Follow this track easily above the crag, to a distinctive **cairn** at the southern end of the ridge. Just north of the cairn you'll see a small stream.

⑤ Follow this down for 10ft (3m) to join a clear grassy track that trends leftwards at first, then follows a clear grove down the spur. This becomes an easy footpath that crosses a broad plateau and then leads to a junction at a wall. Turn right here and drop down to the **Caerfanell river**.

⑥ Cross the stile on your left at the bottom and follow the narrow footpath downstream, past a number of waterfalls. Eventually you'll pass the largest of them and come to a footbridge.

⑦ Cross the footbridge and then a stile to follow the track into the forest. Pass some ruined buildings on your right, and before you cross the small bridge, turn right on to a clear path that leads uphill into the forest with **waterfalls** on your left.

⑧ Continue uphill on the main track, taking optional detours to the left and right to see other waterfalls. Eventually you'll meet a broader forest track where you turn left and then right to return to the car park.

WHAT TO LOOK FOR ⓘ

As you progress along the grassy slopes of the uplands, you'll become familiar with the sight of small, mottled brown birds that flee upon your approach. These are either **skylarks** or **meadow pipits** and although they look similar at first sighting, they can easily be told apart. The skylark is slightly larger, lighter in colour, has a stouter beak and a small crest on its head. The pipit makes a dipping flight, while the skylark is well known for its continuous song, usually performed as it hovers high above you.

The Caerfanell Valley and Carn Pica

Extend Walk 33 to trace the tops of even more spectacular escarpments.
See map and information panel for Walk 33

•DISTANCE•	7½ miles (12.1km)
•MINIMUM TIME•	5hrs
•ASCENT / GRADIENT•	1,706ft (520m) ▲▲▲
•LEVEL OF DIFFICULTY•	🚶🚶🚶

Walk 34 Directions (Walk 33 option)

This short extension crosses a broad peaty plateau to Carn Pica, a giant cairn that offers a whole new vista across the Talybont Reservoir to the Black Mountains in the distance. From here, it makes an airy skyline walk that hugs the cliff tops to cross the heads of two further valleys, before rejoining Walk 33.

Leave Walk 33 at Point ③, where you meet a number of paths at the head of the valley, and take the main track to the right. This heads slightly uphill through an area of peat hags (knolls in deep trenches). Stay on the main track, which is pretty clear on the ground, and cross the moorland plateau known as **Waun Rydd**. You'll locate a small cairn at the path's high point before dropping easily to a huge cairn on the escarpment edge. This is **Carn Pica**, Point Ⓐ. To your left, as you look out, you'll see the cliffs of **Craig Pwllfa**, a perfect example of a north-facing cirque, or natural amphitheatre, carved out of the hillside by the receding glaciers of the last ice age. The grass-covered

debris at it's foot is known as moraine and often acts as a dam, creating glacial lakes such as Llyn Cwm Llwch (➤ Walk 32).

Turn right here and follow the escarpment southwards, where it steepens into significant crags. At the southern tip, you'll see a lovely knife-edge ridge linking the outlying summit of Allt Lwyd. Bear sharp right here to continue along the edge. The path leads to the head of a steep-sided valley, where you'll cross a small stream and bear around to the left to traverse the top of the impressive cliffs of **Gwalciau'r Cwm**, Point Ⓑ. At the end of this delightful section you come to a large cairn on top of a narrow spur (Point ⑤).

If you don't want to visit the war memorial, which is effectively an out-and-back trip, follow Walk 33's descent instructions from here. To see the war memorial, turn right to reach the end of the steep crags, with the memorial directly below you on the left. Locate a faint grassy descent path to the north of a stony stream gully, then drop down to the cairn and wreckage. Once you've finished here, retrace your steps back to Point ⑤.

Walk 35

Around Llangorse Lake

Take a short and relaxing stroll around Llangorse – the largest natural lake in South Wales.

•DISTANCE•	3 miles (4.8km)
•MINIMUM TIME•	1hr 30min
•ASCENT / GRADIENT•	100ft (30m)
•LEVEL OF DIFFICULTY•	
•PATHS•	Footpaths over agricultural land and short road section, 7 stiles
•LANDSCAPE•	Marshy lakeside surrounded by mountains
•SUGGESTED MAP•	aqua3 OS Explorer OL13 Brecon Beacons National Park Eastern area
•START / FINISH•	Grid reference: SO 128272
•DOG FRIENDLINESS•	One difficult step stile, care needed near livestock
•PARKING•	Llangorse Lake, at start
•PUBLIC TOILETS•	At start

Walk 35 Directions

Not all the walking in the Brecon Beacons National Park needs to be strenuous. Sometimes just being among the mountains, rather than on them, can have its rewards. One fine example is this gentle tramp around the lush meadows that hold South Wales's largest natural lake, Llangorse. The lake perches on the watershed between the Usk to the south and the Wye, which runs north of the Black Mountains. Although it's not obvious at first, the lake is actually a product of the ice age, but unlike the typical glacial mountain lakes it doesn't sit

beneath a steep and deeply scooped escarpment. Instead, the debris left behind as the glacial ice retreated trapped water on a hollow plateau above the head of the Llynfi Valley. This water gradually deepened to produce the lake before spilling northwards to form the Afon Llynfi.

The lake is well known for its ecology, particularly birdlife, which is protected by a nature reserve on the southern shores. The water attracts a huge number of wintering birds, as well as acting as a stop-off for species that migrate. The reeds lining the lake also provide an important habitat. One particular inhabitant, a dragonfly known as *Ishnura pumilio*, is thought to breed only in one other spot in the whole of the United Kingdom.

From the car park next to the public toilets, walk across the access road and continue straight across the **Common** on a grassy track. This leads to a small footbridge

WHERE TO EAT AND DRINK ⓘ

There's a seasonal café and bar at the **Lakeside Caravan Park**, near the start of the walk, but if you want to try really good food and drink, pop into to the excellent **Castle Inn** in Llangorse village, which is situated north of the lake on the on the B4560.

over the **Afon Llynfi**. Cross the bridge and bear diagonally left to cross the centre of the field towards another small footbridge and stile. Although you are obviously on level ground, the walk is blessed with great views over some of the surrounding peaks and on this stretch you'll see the sloping table top of Pen y Fan clearly ahead in the distance. Continue in the same direction across the next field until you come to a stone wall, which is vaulted by a step stile. Cross this and maintain the same direction. You'll notice a small copse to your left and beyond this a dense patch of reeds.

At the end of this field, you come to see a wooden footbridge. Cross this and the stile to continue in the same direction again. This leads on to a short boardwalk that takes you through a small gate. Keep straight ahead here, to the left-hand edge of the field, and pass through another gate to continue along the same line.

At the end of this field, pass through another gate and join a broad grassy track at a junction. This is **Llangasty Nature Reserve** and if you turn left here, you'll come to a hide on your left-hand side. To continue, keep straight ahead, passing through a wide gate with two waymarkers on it. Keep left to walk above a small wood and then, at the end of the wood, bear around to the left on another boardwalk, which leads you to a kissing gate.

Go into the wood and cross a footbridge to continue to another kissing gate. Keep ahead here, along the bottom of the field to another gate and maintain your direction to run along a really scenic section of the lake shore – this is a great place to take a break. After passing a few lofty Scots pines you reach yet another gate, by the elegant 19th-century church. This, along with the nearby school and manor house, was built by Robert Raikes, the originator of the Sunday School in Britain. Turn right on to the lane and continue past the school (**Hen Ysgol**) and manor house to a T-junction.

Turn right and continue to a footpath on the right, signposted 'Ty-Mawr'. Follow the track down towards the farm and bear left, immediately before the buildings. Continue along the hedge and turn right over another stile. Head down the left-hand edge of the field, crossing two stiles, on either side of a track, and carry on in the same direction. At the bottom of the field, you'll come to your outward route where you turn left, through a gate, and retrace your steps back to the lakeside.

Walk 36

An Airy Stroll Along the Slender Crest of Y Grib

A strenuous and airy climb on to the Black Mountains via one of the Beacons' finest ridges.

•DISTANCE•	8 miles (12.9km)
•MINIMUM TIME•	4hrs 30min
•ASCENT / GRADIENT•	1,960ft (597m) ▲▲▲
•LEVEL OF DIFFICULTY•	🚶🚶 🚶🚶 🚶🚶
•PATHS•	Clear tracks over farmland, rolling moorland and narrow ridge, quiet lane, 3 stiles
•LANDSCAPE•	High mountain plateau, narrow ridge, steep grassy escarpment, deep and remote cwms
•SUGGESTED MAP•	aqua3 OS Explorer OL13 Brecon Beacons National Park Eastern area
•START / FINISH•	Grid reference: SO 175295
•DOG FRIENDLINESS•	Care needed near livestock
•PARKING•	Castle Inn, Pengenffordd, allows parking for small fee
•PUBLIC TOILETS•	None on route

BACKGROUND TO THE WALK

This is the classic climb on to the highest ground of the Black Mountains. The steep western slopes of the towering massif, accentuated by a succession of grassy arêtes and rounded promontories, hide a multitude of remote cwms that rarely reveal their splendour to the walker.

Y Grib

From the airy ramparts of Castell Dinas, the full length of the bold escarpment unfolds and, while many paths breach its defences, none do so in quite such a dramatic fashion as the one that traces the slender crest of Y Grib. Compared to the gentle standards of this normally rounded and uniform landscape, this narrow grassy walkway feels almost knife-edge in places. Once up, you'll make easy progress through the eroded peat of Pen y Manllwyn and across the top of the boggy plateau to the massif's high point of Waun Fach (▶ Walk 37).

Waun Fach

The line of descent harbours its own treasures as it follows the narrow spur of Pen Trumau, which sweeps gracefully around a deep chasm formed by the infant Grwyne Fechan river. Huge views across the valley show the formidable bulk of Waun Fach as it would want to be seen; the usually understated summit transforms itself into an impressive towering giant that stands head and shoulders above the line of pretenders to its grassy crown. A rocky saddle, steeped in the atmosphere of the craggy peaks that surround it, marks the last of the high mountain scenery. A basic windbreak offers shelter from the cruel wind that often sweeps through the pass and also affords fine views over the expansive Grwyne Fechan Valley, which itself is explored in more detail in Walk 39.

Walk 36 Directions

① A set of wooden steps go down from the back of the car park on the eastern side of the road. These lead on to a rough track where you turn right and then immediately left over a stile. Follow the permissive path down the side of the wood to a stream, cross it and clamber over another stile.

② Keep to the left edge of the field, with the wood on your left, and climb steeply to the top of the field. Leave the wood behind and follow the fence line upwards to another stile. This leads on to the flanks of **Castell Dinas**.

③ Keep straight ahead here to cross the ruins and descend steeply into a deep saddle. Cross a broad track, then climb directly up the steep

WHILE YOU'RE THERE ⓘ

The Normans finally settled on Tretower for their best defence of the pass and in the 13th century built a basic round **tower** on the site of an earlier fortification. The tower wasn't as successful as its owners had hoped and it nearly fell to both Llywelyn the Last in the late 13th century and again to Owain Glyndwr early in the 14th century. The original tower, together with a 15th-century mansion built during more peaceful times and some glorious gardens are all open to the public.

spur ahead. You're now on **Y Grib** and it's possible to follow the faint track all the way up to a cairn and then down to a small notch where your route is crossed by a bridleway.

④ Climb steeply back out of this and hug the crest up to another cairn, where the ridge joins the main escarpment. Don't be drawn off to the left; instead keep straight ahead to climb a short steep wall on to the broad spur of **Pen y Manllwyn**, where you'll meet a clear track.

⑤ Turn right on to this track and follow it up to the boggy plateau on top of **Waun Fach**. The summit is marked by a concrete block that used to act as the base for a trig point; it's now stranded in a puddle of wet peat that makes it an undesirable picnic spot. Turn right and follow the obvious path down on to the ever-narrowing spur of **Pen Trumau**.

⑥ Cross the narrow summit and, as the ground steepens, follow the path through rocky outcrops to a broad saddle. Turn sharp right here and follow the main track as it descends, easily at first. This steepens and becomes rocky for a while before it reaches a gate above a walled track.

⑦ Follow the track down to the road and turn right, then immediately left. Drop to the bottom of the valley and climb out again on the other side. As the road turns sharply to the left, bear right on to a stony farm track that runs between hedgerows. Follow this track past the stile you crossed earlier, on the right-hand side, then take the steps on your left, back to the car park.

WHERE TO EAT AND DRINK ⓘ

The **Castle Inn** has long been a centre for walkers, serving great food and a choice of ales. Dogs are not allowed inside, but there is a special children's menu and extra large portions are available for hungry hikers. The inn also offers bed and breakfast and low-cost bunkhouse accommodation.

WHAT TO LOOK FOR ⓘ

At 1,476ft (450m) above sea level, **Castell Dinas** can safely claim to be the site of one of the highest castles in Britain. Sadly, only a few stones, scattered around the rocky hilltop, are left to tell the story. As is often the case, the Norman motte and bailey style castle was constructed on the site of a much earlier settlement – the original ramparts date back around 2,500 years to the Iron Age. The castle, which guarded the pass now breached by the A479, was superseded by another impressive Norman-built edifice at Tretower, further south. It's a stunning viewpoint and, courtesy of the recently instated permissive path that leads from Pengenffordd to its crown, it adds considerable interest to this excellent high mountain walk.

Waun Fach from the Grwyne Fawr Valley

Take the easiest way on to the highest ground in the Black Mountains above the Grwyne Fawr Reservoir.

•DISTANCE•	9¼ miles (14.9km)
•MINIMUM TIME•	4hrs
•ASCENT / GRADIENT•	1,608ft (490m) ▲▲▲
•LEVEL OF DIFFICULTY•	🚶 🚶 🚶
•PATHS•	Clear tracks over open moorland, indistinct path over boggy ground, steep descent, 1 stile
•LANDSCAPE•	Rolling moorland, deep valleys
•SUGGESTED MAP•	aqua3 OS Explorer OL13 Brecon Beacons National Park Eastern area
•START / FINISH•	Grid reference: SO 252284
•DOG FRIENDLINESS•	Care needed near sheep, 1 dog-proof stile
•PARKING•	Car park at head of lane at start
•PUBLIC TOILETS•	None on route

BACKGROUND TO THE WALK

The high ground of the Black Mountains consists of a 1-mile (1.6km) long, blunt and boggy ridge that runs between the two high points of Waun Fach and Pen y Gadair Fawr. Waun Fach sneaks the gold medal for altitude; at 2,661ft (811m), it stands a less than obvious 36ft (11m) above its shaplier neighbour. But erosion and time has reduced its lofty summit plateau to little more than a shallow peaty scoop that houses the stranded base of a long removed triangulation pillar. This has left the distinctive, conical summit of Pen y Gadair Fawr as the far more worthwhile objective. It's dry, offers great views over the Grwyne Fechan Valley and even comes complete with a tumbledown windbreak, next to the summit cairn.

The Valleys

The real beauty of this small cluster of rounded peaks are the valleys that drop away to either side of the ridge. The Grwyne Fechan Valley, on the western side, is the wilder and more picturesque of the two. It has no road access and its tiny brook is almost permanently in the shadow of the string of imposing peaks that define its western banks. These are explored in more detail in Walks 38 and 39. The valley of Grwyne Fawr is the larger however (Fawr means large or great). Its windswept rolling moorland cradles a large reservoir that provides a scenic focal point for walkers and sightseers alike. It's fed by the tumbling Grwyne Fawr River, a typical fast-flowing mountain stream that rises out of the boggy plateau at its head. The easy angle of the valley means that its grassy floor, penetrated by a good track for most of its length, offers a gentle knee-up on to the higher ground and this provides the easiest approach to most of the surrounding peaks. Lower down the valley, beneath the reservoir, the walls steepen and their wooded slopes provide a short but extremely sharp exit from the lofty flanks of Pen y Gadair Fawr.

Walk 37

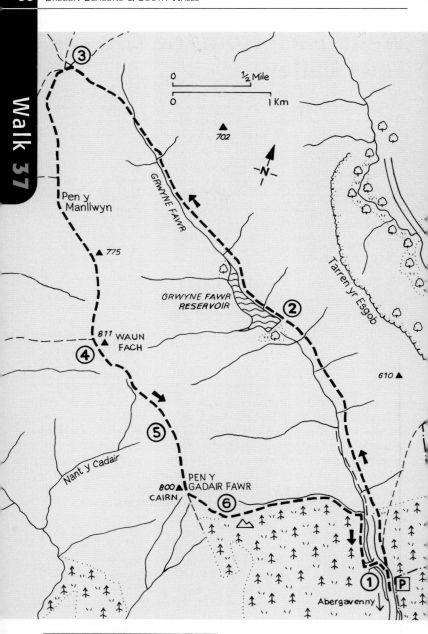

Walk 37 Directions

① Take the broad track at the far end of the car park and follow it out on to the road. Turn right to continue up the valley then, after about 300yds (274m), fork right on to a stony track that runs along the bottom of the forest. Follow this track and continue through two gates to a third gate, by a stand of trees, situated above the **Grwyne Fawr Reservoir**.

② Keeping the trees to your left, carry on past the reservoir and up the valley. Go through another gate and continue until the track finally fords the **Grwyne Fawr stream**. Stay on the stony track, which now peters out to become grassy for a while before deepening into an obvious rut. Continue on to the flat ground above the steep northern escarpment, where the path meets a fence by a stile on your right.

③ Turn left on to a clear track and then, after 200yds (183m), turn left again on to a faint grassy track that leads up the front of a blunt spur. Follow this over numerous peaty hollows to the summit plateau of **Waun Fach**, easily identified by a large concrete block.

④ Continue on in the same direction (south east) across a large expanse of boggy ground. There's no clear path on this section, but there are usually plenty of footprints in the wet ground leading towards the obvious cairn-topped peak of **Pen y Gadair Fawr**, at the far end of the ridge. In the saddle between the two summits, you'll pick up a faint path that initially follows the eroded line of a stream.

⑤ The path improves as it continues, eventually leaving the stream behind and making a beeline for the peak ahead. Climb to the cairn, then continue in the same direction to drop steeply for 10yds (9m). As it levels, the path splits. Fork left on to a faint grassy track that drops slightly and then turns to the right, to the edge of the forest, by a gate.

⑥ Don't go through the gate; instead turn left to head down the steep hillside, with the forest on your right. Follow this path all the way down to the river at the bottom where you turn right, over a stile. Continue along the riverbank for about 400yds (366m), then cross the bridge to the road. Turn right on to this to return to the car park.

The Crickhowell Skyline

Views of Crickhowell and the remote valleys of the central Black Mountains.

•DISTANCE•	8½ miles (13.7km)
•MINIMUM TIME•	4hrs 30min
•ASCENT / GRADIENT•	1,700ft (518m) ▲▲▲
•LEVEL OF DIFFICULTY•	👥 👥 👥
•PATHS•	Waymarked footpaths, clear tracks, 8 stiles
•LANDSCAPE•	Grassy moorland topped with formidable peaks offering great views over deep and remote valleys
•SUGGESTED MAP•	aqua3 OS Explorer OL13 Brecon Beacons National Park Eastern area
•START / FINISH•	Grid reference: SO 234228
•DOG FRIENDLINESS•	Care needed near livestock
•PARKING•	Car park beneath small crag and next to bridge, in narrow lane running north from Crickhowell
•PUBLIC TOILETS•	None on route

BACKGROUND TO THE WALK

This walk climbs on to Table Mountain, which is topped with the remains of one of the most spectacularly positioned fortresses in the land. It then scales the steep escarpment above to cross Pen Cerrig-calch, the highest limestone peak in the National Park. Following a superb lofty traverse that bags another formidable peak, Pen Allt-mawr, it descends a broad ridge that forms the western wall of the beautiful and remote Grwyne Fechan valley.

Table Mountain

Towering above the mountain hub of Crickhowell, Table Mountain appears as a flat-topped knoll tucked beneath the white screes of Pen Cerrig-calch. It is topped by the ramparts of an impressive Iron-Age fort known as Crug Hywel, which translates to 'Hywel's Fort.' Hywel was a significant figure in Welsh history in the 10th century. The grandson of Rhodri the Great, who killed the leader of the Viking invaders at Anglesey, he made huge strides towards the unification of the infant nation and also gained much acclaim for the introduction of a system of rules, which became known as the Law of Wales. The rules, aimed at freeing the common man from the scruples, or lack of them, of rich and powerful merchants, gave improved rights to women as well as placing values on everyday items such as domestic cats. He became known as Hywel Dda, or Hywel the Good. Although Hywel reigned in the 10th century, the fortifications on the hilltop are probably 1,000 years older. It is, of course, possible that he did take advantage of the naturally defended position at some stage.

Pen Cerrig-calch

Standing guard over Crug Hywel is the 2,300ft (701m) peak of Pen Cerrig-calch. It is unique as the highest limestone peak in a landscape that comprises mainly old red sandstone. The name, in common with many Welsh places, says it all; cerrig is stone and calch is lime. Although it appears now to be an isolated pocket of the soft white rock, it would have once been linked to the larger tract south of the Usk.

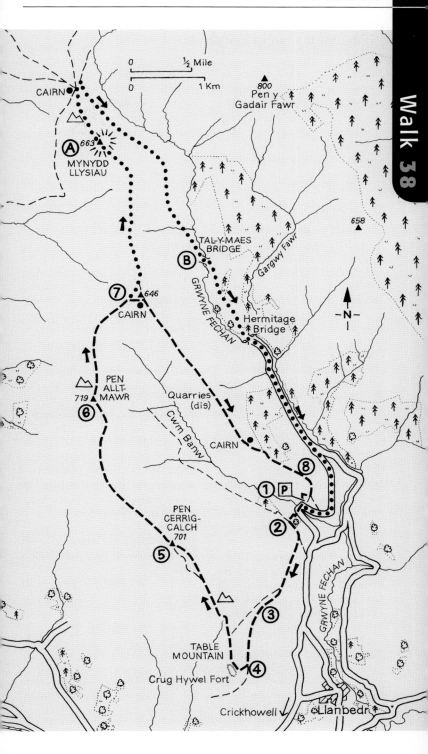

Walk 38

Walk 38 Directions

① Walk back over the bridge and up the ramp that leads to the second gate on the right. Cross the stile and walk up the edge of a field to another stile that leads on to a lane. Cross this and climb over another stile to continue, with a wood on your left, up to yet another stile in a dry-stone wall.

② Cross this and turn left to follow a faint path around the hillside through the bracken. Walk alongside the wall, at one stage dropping slightly, and then, as the wall drops to the left in an open area, turn right to climb slightly to another fork beneath a steep bank. Keep left here to join the wall again.

> **WHILE YOU'RE THERE** ℹ️
> **Craig-y-Cilau Nature Reserve** lies just south of Crickhowell. The main feature is a 400ft (122m) long limestone crag, but there are many different environments within the reserve, including raised bog, woodland and a complex cave system.

③ Continue for about 500yds (457m) to another open spot where the wall dips to the left and turn right on to a track that leads up on to the summit of **Table Mountain**.

④ Turn off the plateau at its narrowest northern point and cross the saddle on an obvious track. This climbs steeply up on to **Pen Cerrig-calch**. As the path levels, ignore a

track to the left and keep straight ahead until you reach the trig point.

⑤ Continue ahead to drop slightly down a small crag to meet the escarpment edge. Continue along the ridge, which narrows slightly, then climb again to the narrow summit of **Pen Allt-mawr**.

⑥ A path leads down the steep northern spur. Take this and cross flat, open and often wet ground towards a small hump ahead. As you start to climb, you'll come to a parting of the paths.

⑦ Fork right here and continue to a small **cairn** on the top of a narrow ridge that leads south west. Follow the ridge easily down until you cross some quarried ground and come to a large cairn. Walk down to a stile at the top of a plantation. Cross this and follow the rutted track down to another stile.

⑧ This leads on to a sunken track, which you follow downhill to a junction of paths. Keep half right to cross a stile and head along the top of the field to a marker post that sends you left, downhill. Bear left at the bottom to a stile by a gate. This leads back to the car park.

> **WHERE TO EAT AND DRINK** ℹ️
> The **Bridge End Inn** on the banks of the River Usk, just outside Crickhowell, does fine food and is a wonderful place to relax on a sunny afternoon. The town has plenty of other options too.

> **WHAT TO LOOK FOR** ℹ️
> The tiny town of **Crickhowell** makes a splendid base for exploration of the area, sitting as it does on the banks of the River Usk and hemmed in on all sides by lofty peaks. There are also remains of an impressive Norman fortification in the town itself. This was built in the 11th century and became famous after it was attacked by Owain Glyndwr in his uprising of the 1400s. The town's most beautiful feature is the 16th-century bridge over the River Usk. Amazingly, it has 13 arches on one side but only 12 on the other!

Crickhowell and the Grwyne Fechan Valley

Extend Walk 38 to explore the heart of the stunning Grwyne Fechan Valley.
See map and information panel for Walk 38

•DISTANCE•	11½ miles (18.5km)
•MINIMUM TIME•	5hrs 30min
•ASCENT / GRADIENT•	1,700ft (518m) ▲▲▲
•LEVEL OF DIFFICULTY•	𝕩𝕩 𝕩𝕩 𝕩𝕩

Walk 39 Directions (Walk 38 option)

This is an excellent extension to Walk 38, adding little to the overall ascent but a few scenically stunning miles to the total distance. It delves deeply into the remote head of the Grwyne Fechan Valley, which feels every bit the very heart of the main Black Mountains massif.

Leave Walk 38 at Point ⑦ by forking left instead of right, to climb easily towards the lower of two humps on the escarpment edge. Pass the boundary stones and drop down to continue north on a clear path that follows the slender ridge. After about 1 mile (1.6km) you'll begin the gentle climb up on to **Mynydd Llysiau**, Point Ⓐ. The views across the head of the valley are wonderful from here, with Waun Fach lording it over the whole scene and Pen y Gadair Fawr staring back at you from the opposite hillside. To your left is the Rhiangoll Valley, penetrated by the A479, and beyond that the distinctive shoulder of Mynydd Troed and the lengthy upland plateau of Mynydd Llangorse.

Drop down steeply from the narrow summit into a large saddle, marked with a junction of paths and a prominent **cairn**. Fork right, on to a stony track that drops easily down to a sharp right-hand bend. The more intrepid may want to carry straight on here to pick up the infant **Grwyne Fechan**, which can be followed downstream to **Tal-y-maes Bridge**. It's very remote and pretty but the going is quite rough and considerably more demanding than the main route described.

Unless you've chosen the harder option, round the bend and follow the broad track down the side of the valley. After a mile (1.6km), meet a dry-stone wall, followed by open moorland again. Eventually you'll drop to the **Tal-y-maes Bridge**, Point Ⓑ, a sheltered and scenic spot that makes an ideal place for a rest. Cross the bridge and climb up the opposite hillside on a good track that then bears right to run easily along the top of a succession of fields. The track then drops steeply through a wood and meets the road head at **Hermitage**. Continue down the road, keeping right at the fork, and after another mile (1.6km), you'll arrive back at the start of the walk.

Twmbarlwm and Cwm Carn

A short but strenuous jaunt through mixed forests to a fine viewpoint atop an historic hill.

•DISTANCE•	2½ miles (4km)
•MINIMUM TIME•	1hr 30min
•ASCENT / GRADIENT•	1,017ft (310m)
•LEVEL OF DIFFICULTY•	👫 👫 👫
•PATHS•	Clear footpaths and forest tracks, 1 stile
•LANDSCAPE•	Steep-sided, forested valleys, far-reaching views from open hillside near top
•SUGGESTED MAP•	aqua3 OS Explorer 152 Newport & Pontypool
•START / FINISH•	Grid reference: ST 228936
•DOG FRIENDLINESS•	Great dog-walking area, 1 difficult stile, care needed near livestock on Twmbarlwm
•PARKING•	Forest Drive Visitor Centre
•PUBLIC TOILETS•	At visitor centre

Walk 40 Directions

It would be difficult to imagine a more transformed landscape that that of the Valleys. Where once slag and spoil heaps towered over bleak villages and greyness appeared to tint everything, there is now every conceivable shade of green, created by mixed forestry clinging determinedly to the steep South Wales hillsides.

The landscapes, once scarred by years of human toil have been given a proverbial coat of paint and returned to the people for leisure. Cwm Carn is only one of many parks in the area that have received this treatment. Its crowning glory, the mighty hill fort of Twmbarlwm, and its incredible views over the Bristol Channel have always been favourites of mine.

From the car park, head past the **Visitor Centre**, keeping it on your left-hand side, and pass through a gate on to a tarmac footpath. Follow this to **Cwm Carn Lake**, which was actually built using spoil and debris from the colliery. Walk along either side of the small lake and then, at the far end, continue up a footpath with the stream on your left-hand side.

Pass a little pond and then, at a timber barrier, cross the stream on a tarmac bridge. Bear around to the right and continue up the valley, with a steep grassy bank, once a

---

WHILE YOU'RE THERE ⓘ

Caerleon is one of the most significant Roman sites in Europe and well worth a visit to see the remains of the centurion's barracks including a well-preserved amphitheatre, of the kind that would have been used to watch the gladiators perform, and a complex system of baths that are remarkably well-preserved considering their age. Caerleon is also believed by some to have been King Arthur's court.

spoil heap, on your left. Above this, you should be able to make out an old winding wheel, which marks the spot of the colliery's second downshaft.

Continue over the stream again (information plaque), then bear right through a gate to walk uphill on a narrow path. This ends at a stile, which you don't cross; instead, take the second track on the left. This leads on to the tarmac **Forest Drive** where you turn right and immediately left, to continue uphill on a broad track.

This emerges again on to the Forest Drive; turn right to follow it down slightly and around a sharp right-hand bend. Fork left here, on to a narrow grassy trail that leads uphill. Follow this to the Forest Drive again and turn right to a four-way junction. Take the second of the two left turns and climb to a stile on the left, which leads on to the open hillside of **Twmbarlwm**.

Cross the stile and follow the track steeply up to a bank and a deep ditch that formed the defensive ramparts of a sizeable Iron-Age settlement. Continue to the trig point, from where there are fabulous views in all directions, then carry on in the same direction to the strange-looking castle mound at the eastern end of the ridge. The purpose of the mound isn't known, but it's considered to be of Norman construction, from around 1070.

Retrace your steps back down to the stile and then the four-way junction where you keep almost straight ahead, down some wooden steps, on to a waymarked bridleway.

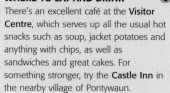

WHERE TO EAT AND DRINK

There's an excellent café at the **Visitor Centre**, which serves up all the usual hot snacks such as soup, jacket potatoes and anything with chips, as well as sandwiches and great cakes. For something stronger, try the **Castle Inn** in the nearby village of Pontywaun.

This drops easily down through the forest to emerge on a forest track. Turn right to the **Forest Drive** and keep left to come off the road and on to another waymarked bridleway. Follow this down and then to the right, near the valley floor, to walk above a fence. This leads to the stile at the five-way junction you passed earlier. Turn left, on to the narrow path and walk down to the gate and the information plaque. Cross the stream and turn left to follow your outward journey back to the lake and the **Visitor Centre**.

WHAT TO LOOK FOR

The Industrial Revolution had a huge affect on the valleys of South Wales. Limestone, iron ore and coal were found in abundance and in close proximity to each other. Villages and towns sprang up almost overnight and the land that loosely forms the southern boundary of what is now the Brecon Beacons National Park was changed forever. By the early 20th century, over 250,000 men were employed in South Wales, working more than 600 mines. The **Cwm Carn Colliery** was originally a downshaft, sunk between 1876 and 1878, for the nearby Prince of Wales Colliery in Abercarn. By 1912, it had become an independent mine, owned by the Ebbw Vale Steel, Iron and Coal Co, Ltd. It was expanded with a second shaft in 1914; an engine wheel, close to the walk, marks the spot. Most of the output was shipped to Newport by canal and from there exported to Europe. The colliery finally closed in 1968.

Castell Coch and the New South Wales

From a fairy-tale castle to a wild, windswept hillside – the new-look Valleys at their scenic best.

•DISTANCE•	5½ miles (8.8km)
•MINIMUM TIME•	2hrs 30min
•ASCENT / GRADIENT•	920ft (280m) ▲▲▲
•LEVEL OF DIFFICULTY•	🚶 🚶 🚶
•PATHS•	Forest tracks, disused railway line and clear paths, short section of tarmac, 2 stiles
•LANDSCAPE•	Mixed woodland and open hillside with views over residential and industrial developments
•SUGGESTED MAP•	aqua3 OS Explorer 151 Cardiff & Bridgend
•START / FINISH•	Grid reference: ST 131826
•DOG FRIENDLINESS•	Care needed near livestock; not allowed in castle
•PARKING•	Castell Coch
•PUBLIC TOILETS•	In castle and nearby Countryside Visitor Centre

BACKGROUND TO THE WALK

A wooded hillside visible from the M4 motorway is hardly the place that you'd expect to find a fairy-tale castle, but at the bottom of the Taff Vale, just a few miles north of Cardiff, is one that will easily rival those of Bavaria. Castell Coch, with its red sandstone walls and conical towers, is worth a visit in its own right, but perched on a cliff top amid stunning deciduous woodland, it's also a great place to start a walk. Conveniently, two waymarked trails run close to the castle and these, together with a labyrinth of forest tracks, provide an invigorating circular route that shows some of the many different faces of the regenerated Valleys.

Castell Coch

Every bit as captivating up close as it is from a distance, this majestic building, now managed by CADW (Welsh Historic Monuments), was built in the late 1870s on the site of a 13th-century fortress. Unbelievably, it had no military purpose whatsoever but was, in fact, a country retreat for the 3rd Marquess of Bute, who at the time was thought to be the richest man in the world and based his empire in Cardiff.

Fantasy Style

Its design, by the architect William Burgess, who also designed St Finbar's Cathedral in Cork, is pure, unadulterated fantasy, with a working drawbridge and portcullis, three circular towers and a dream boudoir that features a lavishly decorated domed ceiling. The grandest of all the castle's rooms has to be the drawing room, three storeys high with a ribbed and vaulted ceiling, further decorated with birds and butterflies. The two-storey chimney piece boasts statues of the Three Fates, which show the thread of life being spun, measured and finally cut. Characters from Aesop's fables are also depicted.

The route away from the woods follows a section of the Taff Trail, a 55-mile (89km) waymarked route that leads from Cardiff Bay to Brecon via the Taff Valley, Llandaff, Pontypridd and Merthyr Tydfil. Most of the trail, including the lower section of this walk, is along disused railway lines, along with forest tracks and canal paths.

From the Taff Trail, this walk follows an airy section of the 21-mile (33.8km) Ridgeway Walk (Ffordd-y-Bryniau). This trail traces a fascinating hill-top line across what was once the Borough of Taff Ely until the local government reorganisations of the mid-1990s. The section followed climbs steeply on to the narrow ridge of Craig yr Allt, a spectacular viewpoint which on the one hand feels as wild as the mountains further north, but at the same time gives a raven's-eye view of the industrial side of the valleys.

Walk 41 **Directions**

① From the car park, walk up to the castle entrance and keep right to locate an information plaque and a waymarker indicating a woodland

walk. Take this path and drop slightly before climbing steeply up to a junction of tracks.

② Turn sharp left, signposted 'The Taff Trail', by a picture of a viaduct, and follow this broad forest track around the hillside and then down, where it meets the disused railway line. Continue along this for over a mile (1.6km) until you pass a picnic area and come to a barrier.

③ Go through the barrier then, as you come to a disused bridge, turn right over a stile, signposted 'Ridgeway Walk'. Take this up to a junction by a gate on the left and turn right. Turn sharp left to zig-zag back across the hillside, where you turn right again. Follow this around to the left again, aiming at the mast and then, as you reach the field edge, bear right once more. This leads up to a narrow ridge where you turn left.

WHERE TO EAT AND DRINK ⓘ

For tea, coffee and snacks, there's a decent **tea room** within Castell Coch. For good pub food, stop on your way round at the **Black Cock Inn** or alternatively, head easily back there once you've finished. To do this, head left out of the car park and bear around to the left at the top of the hill.

---

④ Climb steeply up the ridge and continue, with high ground to your left, to a waymarker that directs you up a narrow track to the ridge top. Bear right and cruise easily along, with great views until it starts to drop. Keep right to drop to another track and bear left on to this.

⑤ Follow it down through the bracken to an open area with a stile.

Cross this and take the track down to a gate that leads on to a tarmac drive. Turn left and continue past some houses on the right-hand side to a junction. Turn right and climb up to another junction, where you bear right.

⑥ Carry on past the **golf club**, then fork right on to a narrow lane that drops and bears around to the left. Turn right here to walk past the Forestry Commission sign and then left, on to a narrow footpath marked by a yellow-ringed post.

⑦ Follow this path, ignoring tracks on both the right and left, until the posts become blue and you come to a T-junction by a sign forbidding horse riding. Turn left here, where the posts are once again yellow, and continue downhill, past a turning on the left to the **Countryside Visitor Centre**.

⑧ The track swings around to the right and descends to meet the drive. Turn right to climb up the drive and back to the castle.

WHILE YOU'RE THERE ⓘ

For me, the most chilling sight in the Valleys are the **arches** that mark the graves of the 144 people killed by the collapse of a giant spoil heap in Aberfan in October 1966. The horrific landslide engulfed the Pantglas Primary School, burying 116 children. Some of the inscriptions on the headstones are truly heart rending.

WHAT TO LOOK FOR ⓘ

Fforest Fawr is a great place to spot woodland birds and mammals. **Grey squirrels** are common and have become unpopular in some quarters due to their inquisitive nature, insatiable appetite and ability to destroy bird feeders – they are frequently referred to as bushy-tailed rats. Nevertheless, their acrobatic displays are spectacular enough to bring a smile to anybody's face. They are often blamed for the demise of the smaller red squirrel in this country, but recent research has shown that the smaller, tufty-eared relative has actually declined due to habitat loss, courtesy of development.

Sweet Walking on Sugar Loaf

Escape the crowds and see another side of the most distinctive of the Abergavenny peaks.

•DISTANCE•	4½ miles (7.2km)
•MINIMUM TIME•	2hrs 30min
•ASCENT / GRADIENT•	1,150ft (350m) ▲▲▲
•LEVEL OF DIFFICULTY•	🚶🚶 🚶🚶 🚶
•PATHS•	Grassy tracks, no stiles
•LANDSCAPE•	Bracken-covered hillsides, secluded valley and rugged mountain top
•SUGGESTED MAP•	aqua3 OS Explorer OL13 Brecon Beacons National Park Eastern area
•START / FINISH•	Grid reference: SO 268167
•DOG FRIENDLINESS•	Care needed near sheep
•PARKING•	Top of small lane running north from A40, to west of Abergavenny
•PUBLIC TOILETS•	None on route

BACKGROUND TO THE WALK

The Sugar Loaf, or Mynydd Pen-y-fal to give it its Welsh name, is without a doubt one of the most popular mountains in the National Park. The distinctive, cone-shaped outline of the rock-strewn summit is visible from miles around and the convenient placing of a car park on the southern flanks of the mountain makes it easy for those who just want to 'climb a mountain'. To follow the well-trodden trade route is to miss the best of the hill, which, despite its popularity, remains a formidable and dignified peak. This walk takes a more subtle approach, leaving the masses on Mynydd Llanwenarth and dipping into a lonely combe, before making an enjoyable push, up the less-walked west ridge. The steep walls of the valley give a much better sense of scale to the gentle giant you're about to climb. The descent follows the more ordinary route back to the car park.

The National Trust

The Sugar Loaf, and some of the land that surrounds it, belongs to the National Trust, who own around 4 per cent of the land within the National Park. The Trust was founded in 1895 with the objective of protecting places of beauty and value from the onslaught of industrial development – particularly pertinent in South Wales. It is not, as is sometimes believed, a government-run agency, but a registered charity that relies on membership and donations to carry out its work. The Trust currently acts as a guardian for over 200 historic houses and gardens, 49 industrial monuments, 612,808 acres (248,000ha) of countryside, including the Brecon Beacons' highest peaks of Pen y Fan and Corn Du, and nearly 600 miles (965km) of coast. It has the statutory power to declare land inalienable, meaning that it can't be sold or purchased against the Trust's wishes without special parliamentary procedures. Wherever possible, the Trust offers open access to its common land enabling walkers to explore at will.

Walk 42

So Many Sheep

Wales has one of the highest densities of sheep in the world. In the Brecon Beacons National Park they outnumber people by 30 to 1. Most of the farms in the National Park are sheep farms, but many also maintain a small herd of beef cattle on the lower ground. The sheep you will see while walking across the upland commons are mainly the hardy Welsh mountain sheep, the smallest of the commercially bred sheep with a small head, small ears and a white or tanned face with dark eyes. They thrive in the harsh mountain environment – the ewes spend as many as 36 weeks every year on the high ground – and are adept at eking a living out of the very poor grazing available. Typically, the ewes celebrate the New Year by being returned to the hill – around 80 per cent of them will be carrying lambs. They're scanned for twins in February and those carrying two lambs will be retained on the low ground with supplementary food until they've given birth. Around April, the rest of the flock is brought down for lambing, then returned to the high ground, with their lambs, by mid-May. In July the ewes are sheared, in August and September the lambs are weaned and the male lambs and surplus ewe lambs sold or retained on lower ground for finishing. By November, the older ewes are 'drafted' on to lower ground and usually sold for cross-breeding with lower level breeds. The young, replacement ewes are also brought down on to lowland pastures for the winter. Late in the month, the mature ewes are also brought down to be mated and the cycle begins again.

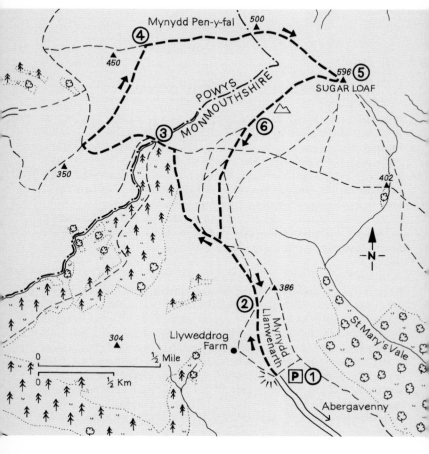

Walk 42

Walk 42 **Directions**

① Standing in the car park and looking up the slope you'll see three obvious tracks leading away. The lowest, down to the left, is a tarmac drive; above this, but still heading out left, is a broad grassy track. Take this and follow it for 500yds (457m) to the corner of a dry-stone wall.

WHILE YOU'RE THERE ⓘ

Between Abergavenny and Monmouth, lies a trio of **Norman fortifications**, White Castle, Skenfrith Castle and Grosmont Castle. They are all managed by CADW and all open to the public during the summer months. White Castle, so named because it was once painted white, is the most impressive and easiest to reach, Skenfrith is in a pretty riverside location and Grosmont sits right on the border with England.

---

② This marks a crossroads where you keep straight ahead, to follow the wall on your left. Continue along this line for another ½ mile (800m), ignoring any right forks, and keeping the wall down to your left. Eventually, you'll start to drop down into a valley, where you leave the wall and head diagonally towards a wood. At the end of the wood, keep left to descend a grassy path to the stream.

③ Climb out of the valley, keeping to the steepest, right-hand path. This leads around a shoulder and meets another dry-stone wall.

Follow this, still climbing a little, until it levels by a corner and gate in the wall. Turn right here, cross some lumpy ground and follow the grassy path up.

④ As the track levels, you'll be joined by another track from the left. Continue ahead and climb on to the rocks at the western end of the summit ridge. Follow the ridge to the white-painted **trig point**.

⑤ Looking back towards the car park, you'll see that the hillside is criss-crossed with tracks. Most will lead you back eventually, but the easiest route follows a path that traverses right, from directly below the trig point. This veers left and drops steeply down a blunt spur.

WHERE TO EAT AND DRINK ⓘ

Abergavenny has plenty of options. For pub grub there's the inexpensive **Somerset Arms** in Victoria Street, or the equally good value **King's Arms** in Neville Street. There are also a couple of decent coffee houses and tea shops, as well as a variety of take aways.

---

⑥ Follow this past an insignificant right fork and then as the path levels, carry straight on at a crossroads. Keep left at another fork, then bear right at the next one to follow an almost sunken track along a broken wall, which leads to a junction by a wall. This is the track that you followed on the outward leg. Bear left and retrace your steps back to the car park.

WHAT TO LOOK FOR ⓘ

You'll notice from the **signage** that Sugar Loaf, and much of the land that surrounds it, is owned by the National Trust. The Trust owns over 9,000 acres (3,645ha) in the Brecon Beacons National Park, including the highest summit at Pen y Fan and the dramatic outlier of Ysgyryd Fawr (▶ Walk 47). This is a large area of land but barely a fifth of the Trust's holding in Snowdonia, where it protects over 37,000 acres (14,985ha) of North Wales's most dramatic mountain scenery.

Llanthony and its Hills

A demanding trek along the ridges of the southern end of the Vale of Ewyas.

•DISTANCE•	9½ miles (15.3km)
•MINIMUM TIME•	5hrs 30min
•ASCENT / GRADIENT•	2,460ft (750m) ▲▲▲
•LEVEL OF DIFFICULTY•	🚶 🚶 🚶
•PATHS•	Easy-to-follow paths, steep slopes, open moorland, muddy lowland trails, 15 stiles
•LANDSCAPE•	Classic U-shaped valleys topped with broad heather-strewn moorland
•SUGGESTED MAP•	aqua3 OS Explorer OL13 Brecon Beacons National Park Eastern area
•START / FINISH•	Grid reference: SO 255314
•DOG FRIENDLINESS•	Some difficult stiles, care needed near livestock. No dogs in grounds of priory
•PARKING•	Narrow pull-in at southern edge of Capel-y-ffin, close to bridge
•PUBLIC TOILETS•	Next to Llanthony Priory

BACKGROUND TO THE WALK

The sheer size of the Vale of Ewyas means that it's best explored in two different walks. The northern reaches are crossed in Walks 48 and 49, while this one tracks south from Capel-y-ffin to loop around the tiny settlement of Llanthony. The scenery is breathtaking, whichever route you choose, but this circuit has the added advantage of passing the ruins of Llanthony Priory and the opportunity of a great pub at the half-way stage. The down side is that the head of the valley is some way to the north so, in order to follow both ridges, you'll have to drop into the foot of the valley and then climb out again.

Offa's Dyke Path

The early stages of both walks follow the same line as far as the crest of the Ffawyddog ridge. From here, this circuit will take you south, over the distinctive serrated skyline of Chwarel y Fan, the site of some disused quarries and, at 2,227ft (679m), the highest point of the day. The ridge then drops steadily down to Bal-mawr, where you'll follow the banks of the Bwchel brook, through Cwm Bwchel, to the hamlet of Llanthony. From the priory, it's up again, easily at first as you cross the fields adjacent to the ruins, but then steeply to gain a blunt spur that leads on to the slim ridge of Hatterrall. Offa's Dyke Path follows the crest of the ridge, as does the border that separates England and Wales. Another steep drop brings you back to the pastures above Capel-y-ffin, where you'll pass two tiny, whitewashed chapels before you reach the road.

Ancient Boundary

In an attempt to keep the Welsh to the west, King Offa, the 8th-century ruler of Mercia (Central England), decided to mark out his borders using a deep ditch and an earth wall to strengthen any natural boundaries such as rivers or ridges. It ran from Prestatyn, on the

North Wales coast, to Chepstow, at the mouth of the River Wye. In places it was over 20ft (6m) high and 60ft (18m) wide.

Although the official border has changed a little in the ensuing years, it still follows a similar line to the original earthworks. Offa's Dyke National Trail opened in 1971. It follows the north–south line of the dyke for 177 miles (285km) and showcases the incredible diversity of the Welsh countryside.

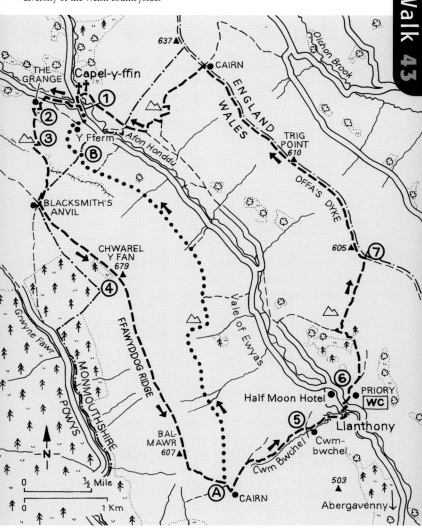

Walk 43 Directions

① Walk towards the bridge, but before you cross it bear left up a narrow lane, signposted to **The**

Grange Pony Trekking Centre.
Follow this past a footpath on the left, marked by a stone archway, to a drive on the left, again leading to the trekking centre. Follow this up to a cluster of barns.

Walk 43

② Keep right here and continue to a large house on the right, with a gate blocking your progress ahead. Bear left and climb up to another gate. Pass through this and scale the eroded grassy bank ahead before turning right on to a clear path that leads through the bracken. This then backs left and crosses easier ground, and the source of a small stream, to the foot of a steep, zig-zagging track that climbs steeply up the escarpment.

③ Follow this track, bearing both right and left and then, as the gradient eases, continue straight ahead on a broad and often boggy track. Continue past a few small cairns to a large one, the **Blacksmith's Anvil**, that sits on top of the ridge. Turn left here and continue to follow the track south over **Chwarel y Fan**.

WHERE TO EAT AND DRINK ℹ

The **Half Moon Hotel** in Llanthony is worth a visit. This traditional pub, popular with walkers, serves excellent food and offers a good choice of beers. It's at the half-way point of the walk, just past the entrance of Llanthony Priory, or on the way back down the valley at the end of the day.

---

④ Walk straight on, along the line of the ridge, to reach the summit of **Bal-mawr**. Go down to the left and pass a good track on your left-hand side. Keep ahead to a **cairn** and then descend to the left. Drop to a fork where you keep right to follow the brook to a crossroads of paths. Maintain your direction (signposted 'Cwm Bwchel').

⑤ Continue through two fields, down past a house, and on towards two stiles. Take the left stile and follow marker posts and arrows

down to a footbridge. Keep walking straight ahead and continue to a gate, then follow the stream down to another footbridge. Cross this and take the lane to the road. Turn left here, then turn right to visit **Llanthony Priory**.

⑥ Cross a stile on the left, in front of the priory (signposted to Hatterrall Hill), and follow the track to a stream, where you turn left to a stile. Continue through a succession of fields and a small copse to reach an interpretation board. Follow the path up on to the ridge and continue to a crossroads; **Offa's Dyke** is where you turn left.

⑦ Walk along Offa's Dyke, pass the **trig point** and continue for another mile (1.6km) to a **cairn** and a marker stone at a crossroads of paths. Turn left and follow the path down around a sharp left–right zig-zag to a wall. Turn right here, then turn left over a stile. Walk down to a tarmac lane and turn right. Follow this lane to a sharp left-hand bend and keep straight ahead, up steps and over a stile. Continue through more fields to join another lane and follow this down, past two chapels to the road. Turn left to return to your car.

WHAT TO LOOK FOR ℹ

The noble remains of **Llanthony Priory** are set against an austere background of mountain and moor. Worship here dates back to the 6th century AD, when St David himself founded a chapel. The building that you see today was constructed in the 12th century as a religious sanctuary for the Norman knight William de Lacey. The atmospheric ruins have attracted much attention from artists, including J M W Turner, who painted them from the opposite hillside.

Views from Chwarel y Fan

An easier way to see the magnificent southern slopes of the Vale of Ewyas.
See map and information panel for Walk 43

•DISTANCE•	7 miles (11.3km)
•MINIMUM TIME•	4hrs
•ASCENT / GRADIENT•	1,250ft (381m) ▲▲▲
•LEVEL OF DIFFICULTY•	👫 👫 👫

Walk 44 Directions (Walk 43 option)

While there's no doubting the beauty of the vale between Llanthony and Capel-y-ffin, Walk 43 may be a bit much for some people as it twice makes the strenuous climb from the valley floor on to the surrounding hillsides. A much easier circuit can be made by following the walk along the Ffawyddog ridge, above Llanthony, and then using an excellent contouring track that returns you gently to the finish. Although it's only 2½ miles (4km) shorter than Walk 43, it almost halves the amount of ascent, making this walk a much more casual proposition.

Follow Walk 43 to Point Ⓐ, beyond **Bal-mawr** and turn left to drop down, around the hillside, on a broad track that leads easily through the heather. You'll pass above two distinct cwms, which drop down into the valley to your right, but keep straight ahead for just over a mile (1.6km), where the path crosses a brook and bears around to the right, past some ruined buildings. The track, which is easy to follow, goes steeply down the side of the small valley and then swings around to the left, where it levels out considerably to cross the steep hillside.

Shortly after this, you'll pass through a pair of metal gates before dropping again, this time to join the wall that defines the top of the pastures. Your navigation worries are over now and the views are great. You can actually see more from down here than you could from the ridge-top path above. Follow the wall for over 1½ miles (2.4km) until you drop to cross a small brook and climb up beneath a dry-stone wall on your left. This wall circumnavigates a strange dip in the ground that makes a wonderful sheepfold and also offers perfect shelter, should you wish to take a break.

From here, continue with the bottom wall on your right until you come to a large metal gate. Go through and follow a rutted track down to another gate that leads into a derelict farmyard. Pass between the buildings, then bear right to follow a drive around to the left and down to a set of gates above a corrugated iron barn, Point Ⓑ. Go through these and continue out on to the road. Turn left to walk back into **Capel-y-ffin**, Point ①.

Walk 45

Abergavenny's Historic Transport Links

Easy walking along a disused railway and a canal tow path.

•DISTANCE•	3½ miles (5.7km)
•MINIMUM TIME•	1hr 30min
•ASCENT / GRADIENT•	160ft (49m)
•LEVEL OF DIFFICULTY•	
•PATHS•	Clear, well-surfaced tracks and paths, no stiles
•LANDSCAPE•	Mixed woodland and tranquil canal banks
•SUGGESTED MAP•	aqua3 OS Explorer OL13 Brecon Beacons National Park Eastern area
•START / FINISH•	Grid reference: SO 262134
•DOG FRIENDLINESS•	Family walkways so scoop the poop
•PARKING•	Small car park at start, south of Govilon
•PUBLIC TOILETS•	None on route

Walk 45 Directions

This delightful little walk, by far the least strenuous in the book, follows the lines drawn by two of the area's main 18th- and 19th-century transport arteries. The outward leg follows the now defunct Merthyr, Tredegar and Abergavenny Railway, often known as the 'Heads of the Valleys Railway'. In places the line follows the path of the much earlier Bailey's Tramroad, which ran from Crawshay Bailey's Ironworks at Nantyglo to Govilon Wharf on the banks of the canal. The initial construction, which stretched between Abergavenny and Brynmaur, was started by the Merthyr, Tredegar and Abergavenny Railway Company. This was then acquired by the London and North Western Railway, who were keen to gain a foothold in South Wales, where they saw the immense profit potential of the 'black gold'. They extended it to Merthyr Tydfil. The

line opened in 1862 and closed in 1958. It now forms part of the Govilon to Abergavenny Community Route.

The return leg winds along the tow path of the Monmouthshire and Brecon Canal, originally known as the Brecknock and Abergavenny Canal. Built between 1797 and 1812, it represents a remarkable feat of engineering, with over 23 miles (37km) of its total 33 miles (53km) being level, amazing when you think of the mountainous terrain that it traverses. Linking Brecon with Newport and hence the Bristol Channel, the canal was used to transport stone and processed lime from local quarries, including the impressive Llangattock Escarpment,

> **WHERE TO EAT AND DRINK** ⓘ
>
> The **Bridgend Inn** in Govilon is a lively, comfortable place, which serves good beer and excellent food that varies from the exotic to its own famous beef and dripping sandwiches!

seen easily from the Black Mountains above Crickhowell. The canal drifted into disrepair by the 1930s but has been restored by British Waterways, with support from the National Park. It was reopened for leisure traffic in 1970.

WHILE YOU'RE THERE ℹ

See some more of the canal by either hiring a boat from one of the many operators or alternatively take a **half-day cruise** from Brecon – Dragonfly Cruises operate from the Canal Basin area near the theatre. It really is a relaxing way to see the countryside.

A clear tree-covered track runs parallel to the car park. Go through the barrier on to it and turn left. This is now the line of the railway. Follow it beneath a bridge to a residential road and go straight across, around a barrier. Continue behind a row of houses and cross beneath the road again. The path then vaults the canal on a bridge that you should note as it marks the spot where you leave the waterside on the return leg. Continue parallel to the canal for a while, then duck back into woodland, keeping straight ahead at a junction, waymarked right to the canal. The path passes beneath deciduous trees made up mainly of oak, birch and ash. You're likely to see many small birds, especially those of the garden variety, including most members of the tit family, robins and wrens.

About 1¼ miles (2km) after crossing the canal, you'll come to a gate and a car park on the outskirts of the small village of **Llanfoist**, which grew up on the transport links of the area. Its lime kilns were fed by limestone quarried on the flanks of Blorenge (➤ Walk 46) and brought down to the canal by another

tramway. Turn right, cross the main road and walk up the lane opposite. This passes the church on the left and climbs steeply up to the canal by the boatyard. The lane swings sharply left and right and then, before you actually cross the canal, follow the signs on to the tow path.

Continue along the bank, which is particularly beautiful in autumn when the magnificent beech woods show off a full spectrum of autumn colours. After about a mile (1.6km), you'll cross a bridge to continue on the south bank, with some canalside houses taking prime waterfront locations opposite. Shortly after this you come to the **Govilon Boat Yard**, where an interpretation board maps out many interesting facets of the canal's history. Govilon, like its neighbour Llanfoist, came about because of its position between the natural resources of the mountains and the developing transport network. It was ideally positioned to receive stone from Clydach, which was then transferred to the canal by tram.

Pass the impressive **boat club** and another attractive waterside building and then, at the bridge, fork left to climb steps away from the canal. This leads back on to the disused railway where you bear left to follow it back into the residential area and on to the car park.

WHAT TO LOOK FOR ℹ

As you walk along the banks of the canal, look out for a glimpse of one of Britain's most colourful birds, the **kingfisher**. In flight, the diminutive little hunter appears less like a bird and more like an ethereal flash of luminescent blue that resembles something from a fairy tale. It nests in tunnels in the riverbank and generally lays six or seven white eggs.

Bird's-eye View of Abergavenny

A short sortie on to the hill that towers above the Beacons' eastern gateway.

•DISTANCE•	3 miles (4.8km)
•MINIMUM TIME•	1hr 30min
•ASCENT / GRADIENT•	530ft (161m) ▲ ▲ ▲
•LEVEL OF DIFFICULTY•	🚶 🚶🚶 🚶
•PATHS•	Clear tracks over open mountainside, quiet lane, no stiles
•LANDSCAPE•	Rugged mountain scenery, huge views over Usk Valley
•SUGGESTED MAP•	aqua3 OS Explorer OL13 Brecon Beacons National Park Eastern area
•START / FINISH•	Grid reference: SO 270109
•DOG FRIENDLINESS•	Care needed near livestock
•PARKING•	Small car park at Carn-y-gorfydd
•PUBLIC TOILETS•	None on route

BACKGROUND TO THE WALK

There's no easier peak to climb in the Brecon Beacons National Park, but there are also few that occupy such a commanding position. The Blorenge – the English-sounding name probably derives from 'blue ridge'– towers menacingly above the cramped streets of Abergavenny, with the main sweep of the Black Mountains leading way to the north. The mountain actually dominates a small finger of the National Park that points southwards from Abergavenny to Pontypool. It's unique in being the only real peak south of the A465 Heads of the Valleys road. It also marks a watershed between the protected mountain scenery that makes up the bulk of the National Park and the ravaged industrial landscape that forms the southern boundary. Typically, its northern flanks boast a Bronze-Age burial cairn and the ground above the escarpment is littered with grass-covered mounds, a remnant of past quarrying. The stone was then transported away on the canals and railways explored in Walk 45.

Y Fenni

Commonly seen as the eastern gateway to the park, even if it sits just outside the boundary, Abergavenny is a thriving market town that owes its success to weaving, tanning and farming. It feels a thousand miles away from the industrial valleys that nudge against its limits from the south. The name, which in Welsh means the confluence of the River Venny, refers to its position at the junction of the River Fenni and the River Usk, but oddly, in Welsh, it's known simply as Y Fenni – the name of the river.

Norman Castle

Abergavenny sprang up around a Norman castle that was built to aid efforts by the invaders to rid the area of the Celts. The Welsh proved far more resilient than the Normans had expected and in the end, William de Braose, the lord of the town at the time, resorted to dirty tactics to achieve his aims, such as inviting the Welsh leaders to dinner and then murdering them while they were unarmed. The castle now acts as a museum with some interesting displays of the town's history. Another of Abergavenny's claims to fame is the fact that during World War Two, Hitler's deputy, Rudolf Hess, was imprisoned here after his plane crashed in Scotland.

Iron Town

Only 5 miles (8km) south of Abergavenny, but culturally and spiritually a completely different world, Blaenavon tells the full, uncut story of industrial expansion in South Wales. With iron ore, limestone, coal and water all found in local abundance, smelting began here as early as the 1500s, but the town, and the huge iron works that came to dominate it, didn't really get going until the Industrial Revolution of the late 18th century.

The colliery, now known as the Big Pit Mining Museum, was founded a full century later than the iron works and only closed as recently as 1980. It has been immaculately preserved and well organised to give visitors a meaningful insight into the industry itself, the conditions that the people endured and the culture that grew up around them. As well as the engine houses, workshops and the miners' baths, a tour, usually accompanied by a genuine ex-miner as a guide, includes donning a miner's helmet to descend one of the shafts to the actual coal-faces. Blaenavon is considered such an exceptional example of industrial South Wales that it was declared a UNESCO World Heritage Site in 2000.

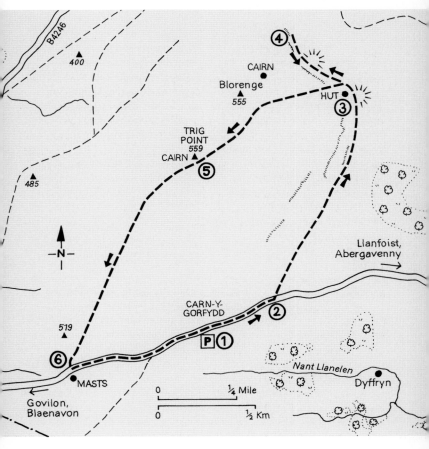

Walk 46

Walk 46 Directions

① From **Carn-y-gorfydd Roadside Rest**, walk downhill for 500yds (457m) and bear left, through a green barrier, on to a grassy track.

② This leads easily uphill, through a tangle of bracken, eventually allowing great views over the Usk Valley towards the outlying peak of Ysgyryd Fawr (► Walk 47).

WHILE YOU'RE THERE
Blaenavon is well worth visiting. As well as the iron works and Big Pit Mining Museum, there's also the incredibly scenic train ride along a short section of the Pontypool and Blaenavon Railway, the highest standard-gauge track in Wales today. It stops off at the Whistle Inn, a nostalgic miner's pub that would have once taken it's fair share of the modest wages paid to the men at the face.

③ As the path levels you'll pass a small **hut**. Continue along the escarpment edge, on one of a series of terraces that contour above the steep escarpment, and enjoy the views over Abergavenny and the Black Mountains. The rough ground was formed by the quarrying of stone.

④ Return to the hut and bear right, on to a clear, grassy track that climbs slightly and becomes stony. Away to the right, you should be able to make out the pronounced hump of a Bronze-Age burial cairn. The path now leads easily to the trig point and the huge **cairn** that mark the summit.

WHAT TO LOOK FOR
This is one of the best places in South Wales to see and hear **red grouse**, which were once managed on these moors. The size of a pheasant, without the long tail, the male is a rusty reddish brown colour and the female more buff and mottled. You'll usually be alerted to their presence by a stabbing, alarmed clucking, followed by a short frantic escape flight.

⑤ Continue in the same direction, drop down past an impressive limestone outcrop and towards the huge **masts** on the skyline. You should also be able to see the extensive spoil heaps on the flanks of Gilwern Hill, directly ahead.

WHERE TO EAT AND DRINK
There are a few good options in the area at the mountain's foot. The **Cordell Country Inn** above Govilon is well worth a visit, especially for the 2-course Sunday lunch, as is the **Llanfoist Inn** in Llanfoist village. There's also plenty of choice in Abergavenny town.

⑥ At the masts, you'll meet the road where you turn left and continue easily downhill, for 600yds (549m), back to the start.

Superb Views from Ysgyryd Fawr

A circuit of Ysgyryd Fawr taking in an enjoyable ramble, a short, steep climb and a fine skyline walk along a slender ridge.

Walk 47

•DISTANCE•	3½ miles (5.7km)
•MINIMUM TIME•	2hrs
•ASCENT / GRADIENT•	1,150ft (351m) ▲▲▲
•LEVEL OF DIFFICULTY•	🚶🚶 🚶🚶 🚶
•PATHS•	Tracks through woodland and bracken, steep climb and easy traverse of airy ridge, no stiles
•LANDSCAPE•	Mixed woodland, bracken-covered slopes, views over Black Mountains
•SUGGESTED MAP•	aqua3 OS Explorer OL13 Brecon Beacons National Park Eastern area
•START / FINISH•	Grid reference: SO 328164
•DOG FRIENDLINESS•	Care needed near livestock
•PARKING•	Small car park at start
•PUBLIC TOILETS•	None on route

BACKGROUND TO THE WALK

Ysgyryd Fawr, or Skirrid Mountain as it's also known, is the easternmost peak in the Brecon Beacons National Park. Isolated from the Black Mountains by the Fenni Valley, it's perfectly situated to offer superb views over the rest of the range. This is a short walk, but it's not to be underestimated; after an easy but enjoyable ramble around the western flanks, the route to the top makes a direct assault on a steep spur that offers little quarter in the fight against gravity. It's definitely worth the effort though, as the summit gives stunning views and the slender ridge that marks the line of descent is one of the finest skyline walkways in the book.

Ysgyryd Fawr

The mountain has long been referred to as the Holy Mountain. The deep cleft in the ridge is said to have been created by a freak bolt of lightening at the time of the crucifixion and the soil in the valley that divides the hillsides is thought to have special powers. It's even been said to have originated in the Holy Land or, at the very least, Ireland, imported by St Patrick himself. History records local people collecting the soil to sprinkle on anything from coffins to fields of crops.

The evangelical importance of the mountain was marked with a small medieval place of worship, dedicated to St Michael, and squeezed on to the narrow summit. Years of mountain-top weather have taken their toll and only the outline plus two small stones that form a doorway remain. There's also evidence of a small hill fort on the same spot.

The name Ysgyryd probably derives from Ysgur, Welsh for 'divide,' and Fawr meaning 'great' or 'big'. You'll find its little sister Ysgyryd Fach, ('small') a couple of miles further south, on the outskirts of Abergavenny.

The Brecon Beacons National Park

Ysgyryd Fawr is the easternmost mountain in the Brecon Beacons National Park. From its summit it is only a few miles to Herefordshire, across the English border. The National Park was founded in 1957 as one of ten across England and Wales. It's the second-largest of the three in Wales, the largest being Snowdonia and the other, the Pembrokeshire Coast. Stretching from Llandeilo in the west to Abergavenny in the east, and between Llandovery and Hay-on-Wye on the northern boundary and the heads of the industrial valleys that define the southern perimeters, the Brecon Beacons National Park covers a total area of 519 square miles (1,344sq km).

Ownership

The majority of the land is privately owned, but around 14 per cent belongs to the National Park Authority, 8 per cent to the Forestry Commission and around 4 per cent is in the hands of the National Trust (► Walk 42). The National Park Authority, which is made up of a committee of both locally and nationally appointed members, is administered in Brecon, with a staff of over 100 people. The principle aim of the park, in common with all British National Parks, is to balance the needs of the landscape and the environment with the demands of visitors and the well-being of local communities. It's a tightrope that it walks very effectively.

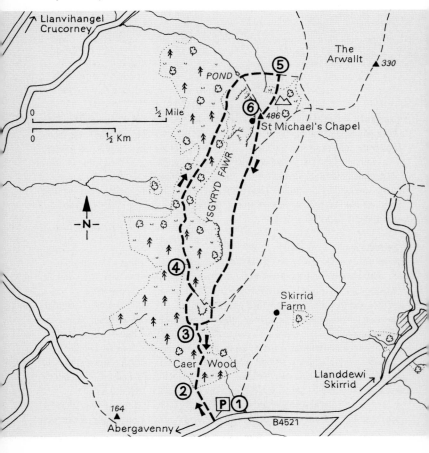

Walk 47 **Directions**

① Walk through the barrier at the western end of the car park and follow the hedged track around to the right. Climb up to a gate and stile beneath a large oak tree. Cross these and follow the yellow waymarker that directs you off to the right.

WHERE TO EAT AND DRINK ⓘ

Considering how remote it is, there's a couple of good options for this walk. East, in Llanddewi Skirrid, there's the **Walnut Tree Inn**, a restaurant with a great 'local pub' feel, and north, in Llanvihangel Crucorney, there's the **Skirrid Inn**, purported to be the oldest pub in Wales and also haunted by the ghost of a rebel who was hanged there.

---

② Ascend a few wooden steps and keep straight ahead at a staggered crossroads, again following the yellow marker posts. You'll cross a grassy forest track and then climb a series of steps to cross another forest track. Continue to a gate.

③ Turn left here and follow the moss-covered wall around. The wall drops to the left, but continue along the path and shortly you'll come alongside a tumbledown wall on your right. Carry on uphill slightly to cross the wall, which drops to the left, and out on to open ground.

④ This now undulates as it contours around the hillside, eventually leading into a narrow rock-strewn valley. Stay on the main path to pass a small **pond** on the left and gradually veer around to the right. You'll cross a small stream and come to an open area with a fence on your left.

⑤ Fork off right here, on a faint path that leads diagonally up towards a prominent shoulder. Duck under a tree at the head of a shallow hollow, then turn right to climb directly upwards. The path becomes clearer as it climbs and you'll cross a couple of contouring vehicle tracks before finally making it to the top.

⑥ Keep straight ahead now to follow the ridge along its length. Drop down the narrow southern spur and bear around to the right to join a stone path. Follow this down to a wall and bear right to return to the gate at Point ③. Retrace your steps back down through the wood to the car park.

WHILE YOU'RE THERE ⓘ

This is the nearest walk in the book to **Raglan Castle**, a few miles east of Abergavenny. Raglan was the last medieval fortification built in Britain and it remains in surprisingly good condition, with an impressive moat and hexagonal Great Tower.

WHAT TO LOOK FOR ⓘ

There are a few places on this walk where the path has been constructed using lumps of local stone, laid in such a fashion that vegetation will eventually re-establish itself around them. **Footpath erosion** is a huge problem across the whole of the Brecon Beacons. Boots destroy vegetation and the thin layer of topsoil is then easily washed away by rainwater, forming deep trenches. It's important to follow these reinforced paths wherever they are found and also to avoid widening any existing tracks by cutting corners or by bypassing puddles and bogs. If you see white bags scattered across the hillsides anywhere, these are full of stone for the paths and have been dropped there by the Ministry of Defence, who use the Beacons for training exercises.

Tackle the Vale of Ewyas Horseshoe

Once you're up, you're staying up, as you trek around the head of the wonderful Ewyas Valley.

•DISTANCE•	9 miles (14.5km)
•MINIMUM TIME•	4hrs
•ASCENT / GRADIENT•	1,560ft (475m) ▲▲▲
•LEVEL OF DIFFICULTY•	杰 杰 杰
•PATHS•	Easy-to-follow tracks, steep slopes, open moorland, no stile
•LANDSCAPE•	Classic U-shaped valleys, broad heather-strewn moorland
•SUGGESTED MAP•	aqua3 OS Explorer OL13Brecon Beacons National Park Eastern area
•START / FINISH•	Grid reference: SO 255314
•DOG FRIENDLINESS•	Great for dogs but care required near livestock
•PARKING•	Narrow pull-in at southern edge of village, close to bridge
•PUBLIC TOILETS•	None on route

BACKGROUND TO THE WALK

The steep clamber up out of Capel-y-ffin (► also Walk 43) will definitely have you searching for breath, but don't be put off. Once you've made the giant cairn that marks the top, the rest is child's play and the views, as you cruise comfortably along the giant whaleback that makes up the Ffawyddog ridge, are just superb.

At Pen Ros Dirion, you nudge over 2,296ft (the 700m contour on OS maps) and reap the fruits of your labour with a sweeping panorama over the Wye Valley. East is Twmpa, often referred to as 'Lord Hereford's Knob', and beyond that, the Gospel Pass and Hay Bluff – the eastern end of the impressive Black Mountains escarpment. The head of the Ewyas Valley is split in two by a rugged slither of upland known as Darren Llwyd. This offers an airy return route with views to the east that match the earlier vista to the west. The spur drops away sharply at its southern tip and your eyes will be drawn straight ahead, where the Ewyas displays the classic U-shape of its ice-age roots.

Book City

This is the nearest walk in the book to the small town of Hay-on-Wye, which can be seen clearly from the northern escarpment. Known as the 'second-hand book capital of Wales', if not the world, the town marks both the northernmost point of the National Park and also the Anglo-Welsh border, with Herefordshire to the east and Powys to the west.

Like many of the towns in the area, Hay-on-Wye grew up around its Norman castle, which was built on the site of an earlier motte and bailey construction. This was all but destroyed by Owain Glyndwr, the statesman-cum-warrior and self-declared Prince of Wales, during his crusades of 1400. These days the town's deepest history is almost forgotten and the colourful municipality has reinvented itself as a bustling, cosmopolitan settlement with an upbeat feel that is totally different from the neighbouring farming communities.

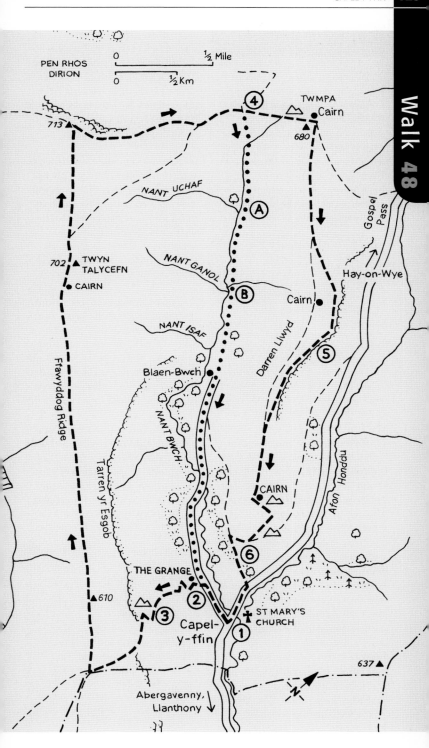

Walk 48

Walk 48 **Directions**

① Walk towards the bridge, but before you cross it, bear left up a narrow lane, signposted to **The Grange Pony Trekking Centre**. Follow this along the side of the stream and past a footpath on the left, marked by a stone archway. Continue to a drive on the left, again leading to the trekking centre, and follow this up to a cluster of barns.

WHERE TO EAT AND DRINK

You have a choice depending upon which way you're heading. Over the Gospel Pass you'll find the cosy **Three Horsehoes** in Velindre, which is well known for its cosy cottage appeal and good food and drink. Or, while heading south, there's the **Half Moon Hotel** in Llanthony village which is definitely a walker's favourite, serving real ale, including the 6 per cent Bull Mastiff, and also offering excellent value for money pub food.

② Keep right here and continue uphill to a large house on the right, with a gate blocking your progress ahead. Bear around to the left and climb on a loose rocky track that leads up to another gate. Pass through this and scale the eroded grassy bank ahead before turning right on to a clear path that leads through the bracken. This then backs left and crosses easier ground, and the source of a small stream, to the foot of a steep zig-zag track that climbs steeply up the escarpment.

③ Follow this, bearing both right and left and then, as the gradient eases, continue ahead on a broad and often boggy track. Take this past a few small cairns to a large one that sits on top of the rounded ridge. Turn right and follow the track easily over **Twyn Talycefn** to the trig point on **Pen Rhos Dirion** (The summit can be avoided by a clear path that traverses left before the final climb.) Turn right and drop steeply down through the heather into a broad saddle.

④ Keep straight ahead over the flat section and then climb steeply up on to **Twmpa**. Turn right here and then, for maximum effect, bear left on to a narrower track that follows the line of the east-facing escarpment. Stay with this track until the ridge narrows and drops steeply away.

⑤ Descend directly to a large **cairn**, then zig-zag, left then right, to cut a steep line through the bracken to a junction with a broad contouring bridleway. Turn right on to this and then fork left, down a steep bank to pick up a narrow stony track that runs along the side of a wood.

⑥ Follow this down to a gate and keep straight ahead to pass between two houses. When you reach the drive, bear left and walk down to the road, where you turn right to return past the small whitewashed **chapel**, to the start.

WHAT TO LOOK FOR

The tiny chapel that you pass at the end of the walk is **St Mary's Church**, one of the smallest in the country, with an interior that measures only 26ft (7.9m) by 13ft (3.9m). It was built in 1762, and the porch was added 55 years later. There are galleries along the west and south walls and an octagonal pulpit. The belfry, which is decidedly lopsided, houses two bells. In recent years, the simple architecture of Welsh chapels has finally become recognised as a significant aspect of the Welsh culture.

Vale of Ewyas: Along the Course of Nant Bwch

Exploring a hidden valley bestowed with many fine jewels.
See map and information panel for Walk 48

•DISTANCE•	7 miles (11.3km)
•MINIMUM TIME•	3hrs 30min
•ASCENT / GRADIENT•	1,360ft (415m) ▲▲▲
•LEVEL OF DIFFICULTY•	🚶🚶 🚶🚶 🚶

Walk 49 Directions
(Walk 48 option)

From Point ④, continue easily across the saddle until, just before you start to climb again, a clear grassy path crosses the track. Bear right here and follow the path down into a narrow niche at the head of a pronounced valley. The track then follows the east bank of the small stream down. The interest on this walk is definitely to your right where, after ½ mile (800m), a narrow, secluded valley hurdles a few rocky steps to empty into the **Nant Bwch**. This is **Nant Uchaf** (Higher Brook), the first of three such tributaries, hewn out of the otherwise barren moorland, that drain into this stretch of the stream, Point ④. The other two are rather predictably named **Nant Ganol**

(Centre Brook) and **Nant Isaf** (Lower Brook).

Just before you reach Nant Ganol, keep a sharp eye open for a pronounced meander in the river. Beside this you'll find a delightfully positioned grassy glade, which presides over a small waterfall. This is as fine a spot for a picnic as you are likely to find in this area. Immediately downstream of the falls, the Nant Ganol makes its appearance, again pouring over a small waterfall, this one framed by birch trees, Point ⑧.

Rejoin the main path and continue down to a gate, which marks the end of the riverside walking. Follow the fenced track down to another gate and a remote farmhouse, where it picks up the road. All that remains is an easy, downhill stroll, back into **Capel-y-ffin**.

WHILE YOU'RE THERE ⓘ

Hay-on-Wye really took off in 1961 when Richard Booth opened a second-hand book shop in the town. Somehow, his business exploded and soon other booksellers set up shop here. Today there are over 30 of them with Booth's being the largest, containing over half a million books. He didn't stop here either. Disillusioned with the inefficiency and bureaucracy of large government organisations that, in his opinion, were doing little or nothing to prevent rural jobs from being lost, in 1977 he declared Hay-on-Wye independent from the rest of the UK, and appointed himself King. The highlight of the town's calendar is the Hay Festival of Literature, which takes place every May.

Break for the Border

Along the valley of the River Wye from Tintern Abbey to Chepstow Castle.

•DISTANCE•	8 miles (12.9km)
•MINIMUM TIME•	3hrs 30min
•ASCENT / GRADIENT•	820ft (250m) ▲▲ ▲
•LEVEL OF DIFFICULTY•	🚶🚶 🚶🚶 🚶
•PATHS•	Excellent, waymarked forest tracks and paths, 2 stiles
•LANDSCAPE•	Steep-sided wooded valleys
•SUGGESTED MAP•	aqua3 OS Explorer OL14 Wye Valley & Forest of Dean
•START•	Grid reference: SO 533001
•FINISH•	Grid reference: SO 534938
•DOG FRIENDLINESS•	Care on main roads, not allowed in abbey or castle
•PARKING•	Tintern Abbey
•PUBLIC TOILETS•	Car park at start of walk and near Chepstow Castle

Walk 50 Directions

The Wye Valley Walk is a 112-mile (180km) waymarked recreational trail that follows the course of the River Wye as it meanders its way between Rhayader in mid-Wales and Chepstow on the banks of the River Severn. By making good use of regular public transport, this walk takes in one of the most beautiful sections, full of historic interest, between Tintern Abbey and Chepstow. The No 69 bus runs roughly every two hours between Chepstow and Tintern and the walk could be completed in either direction although this description follows a north to south line, starting at the abbey ruins.

The best way to join the Wye Valley Walk (WVW) from the abbey is to head out of the car park, the way you came in, and keep straight ahead to hug the riverbank on a narrow walkway that runs between houses and past a small church. This leads up to the main **A466**, where you'll see two small lanes heading uphill opposite you.

Take the left lane (as you look at them) and follow this uphill until it ends and you bear right up a stony track. Keep heading up through a canopy of beech trees until you see a waymarker that directs you across a small stream on the left. Cross this and follow the narrow path up to a stile that leads on to an open hillside. Cross the field to another stile that takes you back into the wood. The path now steepens and carries you up on to a narrow wooded ridge above **Black Cliff**. Keep left as you reach the top, then continue for another ¾ mile

WHAT TO LOOK FOR ⓘ

An alternative route for those with a head for heights involves the famous **365 steps** that lead down from Wyndcliff. To locate them, follow the path from the Eagle's Nest until you reach a junction by a seat. Turn left here, then right at the bottom to the road. Take this to the Lower Wyndcliff car park and follow the waymarkers.

(1.2km) to a T-junction of paths. Turn right, then immediately left and continue above **Wyndcliff** to a fingerpost that directs you down to the airy viewpoint of **Eagle's Nest**. The river curls in a series of giant Us beneath your feet and you should be able to see the imposing limestone cliffs of **Wintour's Leap** on the far bank. These are popular rock climbing crags and also mark the route of the Offa's Dyke footpath, which runs along their tops. Head back up to the main path and continue to a car parking area, where you go downhill, via a series of zig-zags, to the **A466**. Cross the road to the car parking area.

> **WHERE TO EAT AND DRINK** (i)
>
> Most of the establishments in **Tintern** are pretty pricey. Head west for ½ mile (800m), and you'll find the excellent **Cherry Tree** public house, a cosy little place with a pretty garden. It serves excellent food, including sumptuous tuna steaks. Children are welcome until 8PM.

Keep right, parallel to the road, and locate the path, which at this stage is gravel and runs down into the wood. The gravel soon gives way to leaf-litter and beechnuts and the noise of the road is quickly left behind as you delve deeper into the wood. After a short and particularly rough section of path you'll find yourself cruising easily along a narrow terrace above the steep-sided valley. In common with most deciduous woods, there's plenty to capture the imagination at any time of the year, but it's certainly at its best when bathed in the rustic colours of autumn, or in spring when the forest floor is carpeted with flowers and the trees ring with the sound of birdsong. You'll pass behind **Piercefield Park** and duck into a short, claustrophobic tunnel cut into the rock. Continue along and you'll start to head down towards **Chepstow**.

A viewpoint by a bench marks the end of the woodland section of the walk and soon after you'll be directed through a gap in a wall on to a path that leads behind a school and out to a car park. Turn left on to the main road and follow it downhill to a narrow park opposite a turning called **St Marks Avenue**. Turn left on to the waymarked footpath and pass the castle on your left. Perhaps not as spectacular as some other Welsh castles, Chepstow is actually thought to be the first stone-built castle in Britain. The Great Tower Keep was built by the Normans in 1067, just one year after the Battle of Hastings. Take time to have a look around and then turn right by the tourist information centre to emerge on **Bridge Street**, then right to climb up through the **High Street** to the bus station.

> **WHILE YOU'RE THERE** (i)
>
> **Tintern Abbey** was originally founded by Cisterian monks in 1131, although much of it was rebuilt in the 13th century by the then Lord of Chepstow Castle, Roger Bigod. It operated as a monastic settlement until the 1536 Dissolution, when many of its structures were plundered for building materials. Fortunately, a large number of the graceful arches remain intact and the ruin, in a tranquil riverside setting, is one of Wales's most majestic historic monuments. The romantic scene caught the imagination of both the poet William Wordsworth and the artist J M W Turner, although these days, if you want to experience the real tranquillity, it's best to visit at sunrise or sunset and out of the peak holiday seasons.

Walking in Safety

All these walks are suitable for any reasonably fit person, but less experienced walkers should try the easier walks first. Route finding is usually straightforward, but you will find that an Ordnance Survey map is a useful addition to the route maps and descriptions.

Risks

Although each walk here has been researched with a view to minimising the risks to the walkers who follow its route, no walk in the countryside can be considered to be completely free from risk. Walking in the outdoors will always require a degree of common sense and judgement to ensure that it is as safe as possible.

- Be particularly careful on cliff paths and in upland terrain, where the consequences of a slip can be very serious.

- Remember to check tidal conditions before walking on the seashore.

- Some sections of route are by, or cross, busy roads. Take care and remember traffic is a danger even on minor country lanes.

- Be careful around farmyard machinery and livestock, especially if you have children with you.

- Be aware of the consequences of changes in the weather and check the forecast before you set out. Carry spare clothing and a torch if you are walking in the winter months. Remember the weather can change very quickly at any time of the year, and in moorland and heathland areas, mist and fog can make route finding much harder. Don't set out in these conditions unless you are confident of your navigation skills in poor visibility. In summer remember to take account of the heat and sun; wear a hat and carry spare water.

- On walks away from centres of population you should carry a whistle and survival bag. If you do have an accident requiring the emergency services, make a note of your position as accurately as possible and dial 999.

Acknowledgements

From the author:
I'd like to thank the magnificent people of South Wales for their hospitality and the staff of both the Pembrokeshire Coast National Park and the Brecon Beacons National Park for their commitment to keeping such wonderful places wonderful. I'm grateful to series editor Chris Bagshaw for his faith in me, also to Karen and Pam for their assistance with the editing. I owe much to my partner, Steph, who walked many of the miles with me, and also to my old friend Tim for his wit and wisdom on many of the treks as well as his unwavering support for the last 5 years. Finally, I must also express my appreciation to two special friends, Honey and India, who even at their age can make me smile on the nastiest of days and turn any walk into an adventure.

AQUA3   AA Publishing and Outcrop Publishing Services would like to thank Chartech for supplying aqua3 maps for this book.
For more information visit their website: www.aqua3.com.

Series management: Outcrop Publishing Services Limited, Cumbria
Series editor: Chris Bagshaw
Front cover: AA Photo Library/C&A Molyneux **Back cover:** AA Photo Library/J Martin